ES

About the author

Humphry Ellis was born in 1907. After studying Classics and gaining a double first from Magdalen College, Oxford, he taught briefly at a prep school and then at Marlborough, and then turned his hand to writing. After a few years as a contributor, he joined the staff of *Punch* magazine in 1933 and eventually became its literary editor. He started writing episodes for the magazine supposedly from the journals of a prep school master, A. J. Wentworth, in the late 1930s and they were finally collected as a book in 1949. The stories were a great success and proved even more popular in America than in Britain, where Ellis became a contributor to the *New Yorker* from 1954. *The Papers of A. J. Wentworth, BA* was followed by two further volumes: *A. J. Wentworth, BA (Retd)* and *Swansong of A. J. Wentworth*. He has also published two collections of shorter humorous pieces: *25 Years Hard* and *A Bee in the Kitchen*.

The Papers of A. J. Wentworth, BA

Prion Humour Classics

* for copyright reasons these titles are not available in the USA or Canada in the Prion edition.

The Papers of
A. J. Wentworth, BA

H F ELLIS

with a new introduction by
MILES KINGTON

PRION

This edition published in 2000 by
Prion Books Limited, Imperial Works,
Perren Street, London NW5 3ED
www.prionbooks.com

First published in 1949
Copyright © H F Ellis 1949
Introduction copyright © Miles Kington 2000

The material in this book is adapted from articles which
originally appeared in *Punch*

A catalogue record for this book is available from the British
Library

ISBN 1-85375-398-X

Illustration by Jason Ford
Printed and bound in Great Britain
by Creative Print & Design, Wales

Contents

INTRODUCTION

by MILES KINGTON

When this book was last reissued in 1980, the quotes on the paperback cover were ecstatic. "One of the funniest books ever. It deserves to follow *The Henry Root Letters* to the top of the bestsellers" – *Sunday Express*. "A book of such hilarious nature that I had to give up reading it in public" – Arthur Marshall. "Few books have made me laugh out loud quite so often" – Christopher Matthew, *Evening Standard*. "I did indeed laugh out loud till I cried" – Graham Lord.

And it is indeed very very funny stuff. I hadn't reread any *A. J. Wentworth*, BA for years and years till called upon to write this introduction, and I have to say that like Lord and Marshall and Matthew, I fell about laughing, and hooted with strange noises, as A.J. Wentworth got himself into awful scrapes and, by trying to get out, got into even worse ones. I have not indeed laughed so much since I last read a William book.

So why on earth isn't A.J.Wentworth a household name? Why, if Marshall and Lord and Matthew and I split our sides with laughter, didn't everyone else, and why aren't the doings of A.J.Wentworth, BA permanently in print instead of having to be reissued every twenty years, every time a publisher falls in love with him all over again?

Putting aside the ridiculous theory that me and Marshall and the other lads are wrong, I suppose that one obvious explanation is that the action takes place inside a prep school, which is too much of an elitist and old-fashioned setting to appeal to a wide public. I don't go along with this. Geoffrey Willans' *Down With Skool* – also very funny and also recently reissued – is set in a prep school. The most enduring funny part of Evelyn Waugh's *Decline And Fall* is set in a prep school. The Billy Bunter saga was set in a far-fetched boarding school. A lot of the best television comedy has come from a setting in a hierarchical institution, from Dad's Army to Porridge, and you don't have to have been in the Home Guard or in prison to share it any more than you had to have been at a girl's school to appreciate the finer points of St Trinian's.

When you come to ponder it, it is hard to think of many great pieces of comedy which are not in an enclosed setting, whether it is three men in a boat, four boys in the Outlaws, or just a few members in a family, as is the case with so many comedies from *The Diary of A Nobody* onwards. (Don't mention Pooter to Humphrey Ellis, though. He has heard Wentworth, Being compared to Pooter rather too often over the years to be flattered any more.) Indeed, the setting doesn't have to have any particular *raison d'être*. I used to love the setting of Hancock's Half Hour on radio, with Sid James, Kenneth Williams, Hancock, Hattie Jacques and Bill Kerr all in the same house, and it never occurred to me to wonder WHAT they were all doing in the same house....

But as soon as you click on to the school set-up in which Wentworth operates, and register a few landmarks (matron, headmaster, etc) that's all you need to guide you towards the real comedy, which is that of a wonderfully well-meaning man who thinks he has got boys taped, and is constantly being outwitted by them and by the whole of the natural world....

"This morning IIIA were unusually quiet when I went in and I at once glanced at the front legs of my desk. Once or twice since I first came to Burgrove I have hurt myself rather badly through my desk falling off its dais the moment I have leant my elbows on it. I shall always believe, though I have never been able to prove it that this must have been the work of the boys However, the desk looked all right today, but I was still uneasy. Every schoolmaster knows how unnerving it is when the boys sit quietly in their places and watch you in that silly expressionless way they have, and I do not mind admitting that I stood quite still in the middle of the floor for a full minute waiting for something to happen. Nothing happened at all, except that I distinctly heard Mason whispering, 'Rigor mortis has set in'.

"I at once strode to the desk to get my punishment-book, but when I opened the lid a pigeon flew out nearly knocking my spectacles off and giving me a very nasty shock."

That is all it takes to set a typical Wentworth adventure in motion. The pigeon is finally caught. It has a message on its leg. The message reads: "Fly at once. All is discovered." Wentworth is furious when nobody owns up and makes them all write out the message, which he writes up on the blackboard to make sure they get it. Later, in assembly, the headmaster accuses the school of writing silly messages on IIIA's blackboard, and asks the guilty boy to step forward. Wentworth, to his embarrassment has to step from among the masters and try to explain.

Ellis is very good at multiplying the small farcical element which inexorably leads on to worse things, and the way everything hangs together makes it hard to believe that the book was written as a series of occasional pieces in *Punch*.

"It started because I was short of an idea for a *Punch* piece just before the war and decided to write a schoolmaster's statement to a coroner," Ellis told me in May 2000, "trying to explain why he had knocked out a child by throwing Hall and Knight's Algebra at him. From time to time after that when I was short of an idea I came back to the same character, and it slowly built up."

Very slowly indeed, when you consider that over ten years went past (including the whole of a world war) before Wentworth appeared in book form in 1949. But in Ellis's heyday it was considered enough of an honour to appear in *Punch* without worrying too much about books as well. And I get the impression, talking to Ellis today, that being a *Punch* writer was the only ambition he ever seriously entertained. After he attained it that is. To begin with he had the usual round of jobs that a classics scholar has when he comes out in the world and finds that nobody wants a Latin or Ancient Greek speaker. He taught at a prep school for a bit, and then became a classics master at Marlborough School in the early 1930s.

"Weren't you ever tempted, "I asked him, "to stay there and become a highly respected senior classics teacher?"

"Never," he said. "I didn't want to spend the rest of my life counting off the weeks of the terms one by one, just like a schoolboy, or being told which pubs in Marlborough I could go to and which ones I couldn't."

He tried for jobs here and there – nearly got one with Imperial Airways – and also sent a piece for fun to *Punch*. It was accepted. He was hooked.

Ever since, Ellis has done nothing but write short humorous pieces, which is unheard of these days. Even people who are well-known for short piecework, like Craig Brown and Alan Coren, do TV and radio and books as well. But Ellis is perhaps the last surviving member of a *Punch* generation of writers who hid their christian names beneath their initials and just wrote short pieces.

Ellis got on to the staff and stayed there for fifteen years, until Malcolm Muggeridge was made editor, when he resigned in protest, partly because he himself had sort of been promised the editorship.

"Rash thing to do with wife and two children to support" he now says drily. But buoyed up by the success of Wentworth in book form – especially in the United States, despite very few of the readers ever having been to a prep school – he became aware of the American market and started sending stuff to the *New Yorker*, which paid ten times as well as *Punch*, and where he had an acceptance of one in three over the years, and believe me, that is very good.

So, is it because Ellis was a writer for humorous magazines – *Punch*, then the *New Yorker* – that he never became famous? I don't think so. I think it's nothing more than that terrible thing called fashion. Look at the quotes on the 1980 paperback again.

"Deserves to follow *The Henry Root Letters* to the top
...." I well remember the Root letters being a
benchmark of 1980, but who reads them any more?
"Hilarious" – Arthur Marshall. Who remembers
exactly what Arthur Marshall did or said any more ? I
fancy that if we were to reread Root now, the use of all
those current celebrities and topical allusions would
make the book seem not just dated but half
incomprehensible. But Ellis was extremely clever,
consciously or not, and in putting Wentworth in a
setting which makes very little reference to the outside
world he made him timeless.

So here we go again with a drive to put A.J.
Wentworth, BA back where he belongs, up in the top
division of humorous creations. What makes it even
better is the knowledge that Humphry Ellis is still alive
and well in his nineties, and ready for the attempt which
is made every twenty years to get people to realise just
how funny Wentworth is. I hope it works this time. I
don't think he is going to bother to wait around for the
next one.

Statement of
Arthur James Wentworth, BA

My name is Arthur James Wentworth, I am unmarried and I am by profession an assistant master at Burgrove Preparatory School, Wilminster. The Headmaster is the Reverend Gregory Saunders, MA. He is known to the boys as the Squid – not necessarily, I think, a term of opprobrium. He is a classical scholar of moderate attainments, a generous employer and much given to the use of the expression, 'The School must come first, Wentworth.' I attach no particular meaning to this remark.

At 11.15 on the morning of Saturday 8 July, I entered Classroom 4 for the purpose of instructing Set IIIA in Algebra. There were present Anderson, Atkins, Clarke, Etheridge, Hillman, Hopgood II, Mason, Otterway, Sapoulos, Trench and Williamson. Heathcote, who has, I am told, a boil, was absent. It should be explained that though I have given these names in the alphabetical order in which they appear in the school list, that is not the order in which the boys were sitting on this

1

occasion. It is the custom at Burgrove for boys to sit according to their position in the previous week's mark-lists. Thus in the front row were seated Etheridge, a most promising mathematician, Hillman, Mason, Otterway and Clarke. Hopgood II, the boy whom I am now accused of assaulting, was in the middle of the second row. The third and last row was shared by Sapoulos, a Greek, and Atkins, a cretin. I do not think these facts have any bearing on anything that is to follow, but I give them for the sake of completeness.

'This morning,' I remarked, taking up my *Hall and Knight*, 'we will do problems,' and I told them at once that if there was any more of that groaning they would do nothing but problems for the next month. It is my experience, as an assistant master of some years' standing, that if groaning is not checked immediately it may swell to enormous proportions. I make it my business to stamp on it.

Mason, a fair-haired boy with glasses, remarked when the groaning had died down that it would not be possible to do problems for the next month, and on being asked why not, replied that there were only three weeks more of term. This was true, and I decided to make no reply. He then asked if he could have a mark for that. I said, 'No, Mason, you may not,' and, taking up my book and a piece of chalk, read out, 'I am just half as old as my father and in twenty years I shall be five years older than he was twenty years ago. How old am I?' Atkins promptly replied, 'Forty-two.' I inquired of him how, unless he was gifted with supernatural powers, he imagined he could produce the answer without troubling to do any working-out. He said, 'I saw it in the *Schools Year-book*.' This stupid reply caused a great deal of laughter, which I suppressed.

I should have spoken sharply to Atkins, but at this moment I noticed that his neighbour Sapoulos, the Greek boy, appeared to be eating toffee, a practice which is forbidden at Burgrove during school hours. I ordered him to stand up. 'Sapoulos,' I said, 'you are not perhaps quite used yet to our English ways, and I shall not punish you this time for your disobedience; but please understand that I will not have eating in my class. You did not come here to eat but to learn. If you try hard and pay attention, I do not altogether despair of teaching you something, but if you do not wish to learn I cannot help you. You might as well go back to your own country.' Mason, without being given permission to speak, cried excitedly, 'He can't, sir. Didn't you know? His father was chased out of Greece in a revolution or something. A big man with a black beard chased him for three miles and he had to escape in a small boat. It's true, sir. You ask him. Sapoulos got hit on the knee with a brick, didn't you, Sappy? And his grandmother – at least I think it was his grandmother –

'That will do, Mason,' I said. 'Who threw that?'

I am not, I hope, a martinet, but I will not tolerate the throwing of paper darts, or other missiles in my algebra set. Some of the boys make small pellets out of their blotting-paper and flick them with their garters. This sort of thing has to be put down with a firm hand or work becomes impossible. I accordingly warned the boy responsible that another offence would mean an imposition. He had the impertinence to ask what sort of an imposition. I said that it would be a pretty stiff imposition, and if he wished to know more exact details he had only to throw another dart to find out. He thereupon threw another dart.

I confess that at this I lost patience and threatened to keep the whole set in during the afternoon if I had any more trouble. The lesson then proceeded.

It was not until I had completed my working-out of the problem on the board that I realized I had worked on the assumption – of course ridiculous – that I was *twice* my father's age instead of *half*. This gave the false figure of minus 90 for my own age. Some boy said, 'Crikey!' I at once whipped round and demanded to know who had spoken. Otterway suggested that it might have been Hopgood II talking in his sleep. I was about to reprimand Otterway for impertinence when I realized that Hopgood actually was asleep and had in fact, according to Williamson, been asleep since the beginning of the period. Mason said, 'He hasn't missed much, anyway.'

I then threw my *Hall and Knight*. It has been suggested that it was intended to hit Hopgood II. This is false. I never wake up sleeping boys by throwing books at them, as hundreds of old Burgrove boys will be able to testify. I intended to hit Mason, and it was by a mischance which I shall always regret that Hopgood was struck. I have had, as I told my Headmaster, a great deal to put up with from Mason, and no one who knows the boy blames me for the attempt to do him some physical violence. It is indeed an accepted maxim in the Common Room that physical violence is the only method of dealing with Mason which produces any results; to this the Headmaster some time ago added a rider that the boy be instructed to remove his spectacles before being assaulted. That I forgot to do this must be put down to the natural agitation of a mathematics master caught out in an error. But I blame myself for it.

I do not blame myself for the unfortunate stunning of Hopgood II. It was an accident. I did all I could for the boy when it was discovered (I think by Etheridge) that he had been rendered unconscious. I immediately summoned the Headmaster and we talked the matter over. We agreed that concealment was impossible and that I must give a full account of the circumstances to the police. Meanwhile the work of the school was to go on as usual; Hopgood himself would have wished it. The Headmaster added that in any case the School must come first.

I have made this statement after being duly cautioned, of my own free will and in the presence of witnesses. I have read it through three times with considerable satisfaction, and am prepared to state on oath that it is a true and full account of the circumstances leading up to the accident to Hopgood II. I wish only to add that the boy is now none the worse for the blow, and has indeed shown increased zeal for his studies since the occurrence.

(*Signed*) A. J. Wentworth, BA

July 1939

Christmas Term 1938
A Routine Week

MONDAY

This has been an unsatisfactory day. When I entered Classroom 4 after break I found the whole class clustered round my desk and immediately ordered them sharply to go to their places and open their books. 'Didn't you hear the bell?' I cried. 'It went two minutes ago.' Some of the boys turned round as I spoke, and I saw to my surprise that they were not IIIA, as I had expected, but the Upper Fourth, and that the Headmaster was seated at the desk correcting their exercises. I am not at all convinced that it is a wise practice to call all the boys up when one is correcting. I have tried it myself with IIIA and also with the Lower Third for English History and it does not work. The boys are inclined to jostle for places, and on one occasion IIIA pushed my desk, through over-keenness, right off its dais, with the result that a great deal of ink was spilled and Etheridge, the best worker of the lot, sprained his wrist and had to go up to Matron. But of course a headmaster has the right to do as he likes.

7

As soon as I realized my mistake I apologized.

'I beg your pardon, Headmaster,' I said, colouring, 'I was thinking it was Monday.'

'It *is* Monday, Mr Wentworth,' he said kindly.

There was no more to be said, so I apologized again and withdrew. I should have remembered that on Mondays I take IIIA in Room 6, since the Library, where the Headmaster ordinarily takes the Upper Fourth, is wanted by Miss Coombes for her Music now that the Music Room is used for P.T. on wet days.

On my way down the corridor to Room 6 I remembered that I had forgotten to bring IIIA's corrected books with me and hurried back to the Common Room to get them. There I found Gilbert smoking a pipe. 'Hullo, A.J.,' he said. 'I thought you were having fun with IIIA this period.' I explained that I was looking for some exercise-books and asked if he had seen them.

'There were some old books on the table this morning,' he said; 'but I burnt those. I thought they were finished with.'

I was nearly taken in for a moment, but I know C.G. of old. 'You're pulling my leg, C.G.,' I said, doubling up my fists in pretended anger; and sure enough soon found my books at the back of my locker.

This incident delayed me still further, and in my haste to get to work I inadvertently returned to Room 4 instead of Room 6. Not wishing, naturally,

to disturb the Headmaster a second time, I closed
the door again as quietly as I could the moment I
heard his voice conjugating the imperfect subjunc-
tive passive of '*audio*', but even so could not help
hearing him say, 'See who that was, Briggs.' I now
made what proved to be the fatal mistake of
running into the boot-room. This little room, in
which, as the name implies, the boys keep their
boots and shoes, lies on the right of a narrow
passage running off the main corridor almost
opposite Classroom 4, and it was natural that it
should come into my mind, since the main corridor
itself continues for a considerable distance on
either side of Room 4 without offering concealment of any kind.

Time and again I have warned the school boot-
boy not to leave the large basket, in which he
collects the soiled shoes for cleaning, in the middle
of the boot-room floor. It is an unnecessary
obstruction, and what is more I have known boys
turn it upside-down and hide under it when I have
been marshalling them for a Sunday afternoon
walk. But the boot-boy has, I am afraid, about as
much sense as Atkins, who is easily the stupidest of
my IIIA boys. I fell over, and indeed into, this
basket with a considerable noise, and in so doing
lost hold of my exercise-books, which flew all over
the room. I was still in this ludicrous position,
striving to free my gown which had caught in the
wickerwork, when Briggs put his head round the

door, said 'Golly!' and disappeared again, no doubt to report what he had seen to the Headmaster.

It can be imagined that I was in no mood after this to stand any nonsense from anybody, and IIIA found that they had a very different person to deal with this morning from their usual good-natured master. I kept Anderson standing up for twenty minutes and gave Mason the shock of his life by setting him fifty lines for singing. A little severity now and then does them no harm at all.

The Headmaster sent for me after lunch and was very decent about it, though obviously displeased.

'I understand, Wentworth,' he said, 'that you were seen sitting in a basket in the boot-room this morning at a time when you should have been supervising the work of one of your mathematical sets?'

I nodded my head and said eagerly that I could explain.

He said, 'No explanation is necessary. I do not make it my business, as you know, to pry into the affairs of my masters. I trust you all implicitly. But I must make it clear that I cannot allow any master to fritter away, in the boot-room or anywhere else, time which should be devoted to the instruction of my boys. That is what we are all here for – to teach.'

I told him that I was extremely sorry for what had occurred, and added that I was prepared, if he wished it, to give an undertaking never to enter the boot-room again. He replied that he did not wish it, that he hoped I had enough self-control to make such an undertaking unnecessary, and that he had no objection whatever to my going into the boot-room whenever I wished provided that neither the work of the boys nor the dignity of my position was endangered by my presence there. He then said that the School must come first, and I realized that the interview was at an end.

On my way back to the Common Room I met Mason and let him off his imposition. It had worried me to think that I might perhaps have let a momentary irritation override my sense of fair play.

TUESDAY

Every mathematics master dreads the day when he will have to explain the Theorem of Pythagoras to boys who have never met it before. Term after term I get this same feeling of helplessness. The whole thing is ridiculous. With co-operation and proper attention even a dull form should be able to grasp the principles involved and the main lines of the proof in an hour's good hard work; knowledge of the construction will come with practice. But IIIA do *not* co-operate. They are too prone to let their minds wander, to be led astray by what are from the point of view of geometry only side-issues, to *make*, as I am always telling them, difficulties instead of going straight at the task and getting it done. It is not that they are lazy. That I could deal with, for I come down like a ton of bricks on idleness in any shape or form. It is rather, I think, a failure to understand the *importance* of what it is we are trying to do.

'This morning,' I said to them, 'we are going to prove that the square on the hypotenuse of a right-angled triangle is equal to the sum of the squares on the other two sides.'

'Is that a likely thing to happen?' Mason asked.

I told the others to be quiet and asked Mason what he meant.

'I mean is a right-angled triangle likely to have a square on its hypotenuse?'

'I'm afraid I don't quite follow you, Mason,' I said. 'If I draw a right-angled triangle on the board and then draw a square on the side opposite the right angle, it has got a square on its hypotenuse. The question whether it is *likely* to have such a square does not arise.'

'Not on the board, sir, no. But I mean in real life. I mean if real-life triangles don't have squares on their hypotenuses there wouldn't be much point in proving that they are equal to whatever it is they are equal to, would it, sir?'

'You mean "would *there*", you chump.'

'Be quiet, Etheridge,' I said.

'I see what Mason means, sir,' said Hillman. 'I mean it would be a pretty good fluke if a triangle had squares on all its three sides at once, wouldn't it, sir?'

'There is no question of a fluke about it,' I said, beginning to lose patience. 'Now attend to me, all of you.' I then drew on the board a right-angled triangle ABC, and on the sides AB, AC and BC proceeded to construct squares ABDE, ACFG and BCHJ respectively.

'What is there funny about that, Atkins?' I asked when I had finished.

'Nothing,' he said.

'Then why laugh?'

It is a constant vexation to me that these boys seem to be amused at nothing at all. I do not want them to be glum and dispirited, of course; there are times when we all have a good laugh together and no harm is done. But this inane giggling at nothing simply holds up the work of the set. I gave Atkins a sharp warning and turned to Mason.

'Now, Mason,' I said, 'that wasn't very difficult, was it? My triangle's got squares on each of its sides.'

'My canary's got circles under its eyes,' sang a voice, and there was an immediate outburst of laughter at this piece of downright impertinence.

'Was that you, Williamson?' I demanded sternly.

'No, sir.'

'Then who was it?'

There was no reply.

'Filthy Dick passed the window just then, sir,' suggested Clarke, who sits by it. 'It must have been him.'

13

'He,' said Etheridge.

'You shut up, Etheridge. You don't know everything.'

'Clarke,' I cried, 'you will come and see me at the end of the period. And you too, Etheridge. I will not have these interruptions.'

'He meant the gardener's boy,' explained Mason. 'We call him Filthy Dick because he never washes. You should see his neck.'

'Never mind that now, Mason. The point is, are you prepared to admit that this figure on the board is a triangle with squares on each of its sides?'

'I suppose so, sir. Only it looks more like three squares joined together now, with a space in the middle.'

'Very well, Mason,' I said wearily. 'Let us put it that when three squares have their corners touching in such a way that the space enclosed between them is a right-angled triangle, the largest square is equal to the sum of the two smaller squares. Will that satisfy you?'

'All right by me, sir,' said Mason.

'Anything to get rid of the hypotenuse,' said Anderson.

I threw my chalk into a corner and went quietly to my desk. 'You will all,' I said, 'open your books and copy out the construction and proof of the Theorem of Pythagoras. Any boy who has not finished when the bell rings will complete the work in his spare time and show it up to me during break tomorrow morning. I am thoroughly dissatisfied with the behaviour of the whole set. Unless there is a decided improvement in the next few days you will find yourselves in pretty serious trouble. Now get on with your work in silence. Well Atkins, what is it?'

'I think Sapoulos is crying again, sir.'

The Greek boy Sapoulos is a source of continual worry to me. The slightest thing seems to upset him. Naturally one makes allowances, as he is a stranger in a strange land and may often feel rather lonely, but it is quite ridiculous that he should break down over the most trivial matters in the way he does. I have tried being kind to him but it only seems to make matters worse, and I dare say what he really needs is a little sterness and discipline. Something to stiffen him up. On this occasion I told him not to be so silly, and asked him what the Spartans at Thermopylae would have thought of such a cry-baby.

I had forgotten, until Mason asked me what the Spartans did at Thermopylae, that none of my IIIA boys knows any Greek history. I told him how Leonidas and his gallant three hundred held a mighty Persian host at bay for days and finally died at their post rather than surrender.

'What were the Persians up to?' asked Etheridge.

I told him of Xerxes' plans to conquer Greece, and, as the boys were obviously interested, went on to describe the marshalling of the great army, the digging of the canal at Athos, the lashing of the Hellespont with chains and the building of the bridge of boats, and how Xerxes wept to think that of all his host not one man would be alive when a hundred years had passed by. I had got Xerxes as far as Therma, where the river Echeidorus was drunk dry, when to my great disappointment the bell rang. I think the boys were disappointed too, for they asked me quite eagerly to go on with the story another time.

Tomorrow we must have a real go at Pythagoras. I might begin perhaps by telling them something of the man himself and his position in the hierarchy of Greek philosophers.

WEDNESDAY

This morning IIIA were unusually quiet when I went in and I at once glanced at the front legs of my desk. Once or twice since I first came to Burgrove I have hurt myself rather badly through my desk falling off its dais the moment I have leant my elbows on it. I shall always believe, though I have never been able to prove it, that this must have been the work of the boys. Old Poole, who left us last year after twenty-seven years' faithful service in charge of French and Geography, had the same experience, and he was positive that the front legs had been balanced deliberately on the very edge of the dais. Though, as he used to say, it might simply be carelessness on the part of the cleaner. It is always difficult to bring this kind of thing home to the boys.

However, the desk looked all right today, but I was still uneasy. Every schoolmaster knows how unnerving it is when the boys sit quietly in their places and watch you in that silly expressionless way they have, and I do not mind admitting that I stood quite still in the middle of the floor for a full minute waiting for something to happen. Nothing happened at all except that I distinctly heard Mason whispering, '*Rigor mortis* has set in.'

I at once strode to the desk to get my punishment-book, but when I opened the lid a pigeon flew out, nearly knocking my spectacles off and giving me, naturally enough, a very nasty shock. In my seven years at Burgrove I have never had such a thing happen to me. I went white with anger.

'Stop that noise this instant!' I shouted. 'And you, Mason, leave that bird alone and go back to your desk. Now, which of you is responsible for this? Hurry up, I'm waiting.'

There was absolute silence for some seconds, until the pigeon, which had settled on top of the blackboard, began to coo in an annoying way, and I then brought my fist down with a crash on the desk.

'We had better understand one another,' I said with cold fury. 'Somebody put that pigeon in my desk and I am going to find out who did it. Unless the person responsible owns up within three minutes – Ah, Mason, so it *was* you?'

'Me, sir. No, sir. Only I think –'

'Well?'

'I think it's got something tied to its leg.'

Someone suggested it might be a message.

'It's a stool-pigeon!' cried Clarke.

'I bet it's spies.'

'Atkins saw a man just like Hitler behind the pavvy –'

'Be quiet !' I shouted.

While I was considering what to do, Mason, who seems utterly unable to hold his tongue for two seconds, asked whether he might find out what the message said. I asked him rather sarcastically how he proposed to catch the pigeon, and before I could object he went to the blackboard and held out his right index finger, which the bird at once settled upon. I gave Hillman fifty lines for clapping, as a warning to the others, and then suggested to Mason that he seemed to know the pigeon remarkably well. He replied that he knew all the school pigeons well and he thought this must be one of them. I had already guessed this, but said nothing.

'Shall I read the message, sir?' he asked, untying it from the bird's leg.

'Very well,' I said, after a moment's hesitation. 'What does it say?'

'It says "Fly at once. All is discovered."'

In the ordinary way I might have joined in the general laughter, but this morning I felt too upset and angry.

'Give me that paper, Mason,' I said, 'and sit down. No – let that bird out of the window first. I want every boy – give out some slips, Etheridge, please, there is no need to waste a whole sheet – I want every boy to copy out what is written here and sign his name beneath it. And no talking.'

'Need *I* do it, sir?'

'Certainly you must do it, Sapoulos. And stop that silly whimpering this instant.'

The boys then began clamouring that they had forgotten the message, and to save further trouble I wrote it up on the board. My plan was of course to compare the handwriting on the slips of paper with that on the original paper; in this way I felt certain of being able to spot the culprit, though as a matter of fact, when I looked through the slips this evening I found that the boys had misunderstood my intention and written the words in capitals, which made the test practically useless. Etheridge collected the slips without incident and I then told the whole set to get on with the solving of brackets in Exercise 37. I felt too weary and disheartened to do any actual teaching.

Unless someone has owned up by tomorrow morning I shall have to take severe measures. But it is difficult to know what to do.

THURSDAY

There was an unfortunate sequel to the pigeon affair this morning. After prayers in Big School the Headmaster said he had something serious to say. It appears that when he entered Classroom 4 for the second period yesterday morning he found what he described as an impertinent message scrawled up on the board. He did not propose to repeat the message, as the boy responsible would know very well what he meant. Let that boy stand up at once and confess. I had no option but to come forward from my place with the other masters and explain that I had myself written the sentence and that I regretted the board had not been cleaned at the end of the period by the bottom boy of the set, whose duty it was. I added, for I did not wish to get Sapoulos into trouble, that the boy concerned had not yet perhaps had time to get used to our English ways and customs.

This ended the matter for the time being, but it has put me in something of a dilemma. The Headmaster, who is, if anything, a shade too inquisitive, will no doubt require a fuller explanation, and though I have managed to avoid him for the whole of today, I cannot hope to do so indefinitely. The difficulty is that I do not wish to tell him about the pigeon in my desk; it would only worry him and could do no good. He is still rather upset, to tell the truth, about my accident in the boot-room. So I shall have to think of some other reason for writing that absurd message on the board. It would be better of course if I could link it up in some way with algebra. But I don't at the moment see my way.

In the meantime I have told IIIA that I have decided to say no more about the pigeon provided nothing of the sort happens again, and I have warned them that the less they say about it to anyone the better it will be for them.

It looks as if I may have to go to the Headmaster over this row with Gilbert about his wretched potatoes. Important as his crop may be, there are other things in the world besides potatoes, as I told him. The boys did not come here, as far as I am aware, to learn potato-lifting, nor have their parents expressed a particular desire to have this subject included in the curriculum. If they had, we should very soon see it down as an Extra.

The whole thing is simply a matter of principle. If it is necessary, in the interests of discipline, to keep boys in for half an hour after lunch, then they must be kept in. The fact that Gilbert has put their names down for potato-lifting at that time is neither here nor there. He must get substitutes. Or he must lift his infernal crop at some other time. It is absolute nonsense to say that my boys get themselves kept in on purpose to miss potato-lifting. Extra school with me is no picnic, I can assure him.

Gilbert made me very angry by trying to argue that nothing was gained by keeping boys in, anyway. I told him, pretty sharply, to mind his own business. Let him use his own methods, and have the goodness to allow me to continue to use mine. Of course if he runs his 'Potato Gang', as he calls it, so badly that they will do anything to get out of it, that is another matter and is an additional argument for my speaking to the Head. His answer to this was that I could go and cry on the old Squid's shoulder all night for all he cared, and he hoped I should be rewarded by having the responsibility for the potatoes handed over to me. 'Then,' he went on (and this is what I cannot forgive), 'when your IIIA boys bombard you with ink-pots again you can give the whole lot an extra hour on the potatoes, thus killing two birds with one stone.'

I went white with anger. Even had any ink-pots been thrown, which of course was not the case, it would have been in the worst possible taste for Gilbert to refer to it. It is an unwritten law among schoolmasters not to allude in any way to any disciplinary difficulties that a colleague may be meeting in the course of his school duties. Naturally one is aware sometimes, one cannot help being aware, that another master is failing to maintain strict order in his classroom. The noise in poor old Poole's room, towards the close of his time here, used to be indescribable. But one does *not* mention it, least of all to the man himself. Gilbert, in his proper senses, knows this as well as I do, just as he knows that it is nonsense to suggest that I, of all people, would allow ink-pots to be thrown about in my room. The fact is, he had lost his temper and was trying to make capital out of an accident that happened yesterday morning in my Algebra period – an accident that happened, moreover, *after* I had been obliged to tell the boys to come in for half an hour after lunch, and so had nothing to do with their punishment at all.

I kept them in, as a matter of fact, because they were rather silly and over-excited about taking out some brackets. I was showing them that the way to get rid of the brackets in an expression like $(a+b)(a-b)$ was to multiply out, resulting in a^2-b^2, when Mason, who is rather a thorn in my side in some ways, objected that in the previous Algebra period we had started with a^2-b^2 and got it to $(a+b)(a-b)$.

'Yes, Mason?' I said, not quite understanding what he was driving at.

'Well, sir, now we have started with $(a+b)(a-b)$ and got it to a^2-b^2.'

'Exactly. That shows we were right yesterday, doesn't it?'

'Yes, sir, but there doesn't seem any end to it. When it's a^2-b^2 we have to work away and get it to $(a+b)(a-b)$ and when it is $(a+b)(a-b)$ you're still not satisfied, sir, and we have all the trouble of making it into a^2-b^2 again, sir. Couldn't we jolly well make up our minds which is best and leave it alone, sir?'

Another boy shouted, 'It's not fair, sir,' and in a moment the whole set was talking at once, urging me to 'make up my mind' and 'leave well alone', and a lot more extravagant nonsense. One boy even had the impertinence to offer odds of three to one on a^2-b^2.

When the whole form forgets itself, it is worse than useless to try to pick out particular offenders. Jump on the whole lot and teach them a good lesson. Half an hour extra does them no real harm. I used it, in this case, to explain clearly to them why it is that sometimes one wants to factorize an expression and sometimes to resolve or simplify it, taking instances from problems in real life. They rather enjoyed it, I think.

In any case, all this had nothing whatever to do with the ink-pots which Gilbert saw on the floor round my desk when he looked in to borrow my dictionary at the end of the period. I had thrown them there myself, if he only knew – for reasons I may jot down here later on, but which I certainly do not feel called upon to explain to him.

We are not on speaking terms at present, which I always think a pity on a small staff, particularly as Miss Coombes, – however, there is no need to go into that now.

FRIDAY

Gilbert and Rawlinson were talking about discipline in the Common Room the other day, when we were all hanging up our gowns after morning school, and Rawlinson suddenly said, 'You'd better ask A.J. about that. He's the expert on lines in these parts.'

'I see nothing to laugh at in that, Rawlinson,' I said, colouring up, and I added that, although I very much disliked giving impositions, it was sometimes necessary in order to keep the boys up to concert pitch.

'Your IIIA lot were at concert pitch all right this morning,' said Gilbert. 'I heard them from the Library.'

'Anyway, Rawlinson,' I said, ignoring Gilbert, who is inclined at times to let his tongue run away with him, 'I think it better to set a few lines than to keep a whole form in on a fine afternoon, as some people do.'

Rawlinson, knowing very well what I meant, replied that he had kept the Lower Fourth in because they seemed incapable of learning the second page of principal parts, not because they had tied his boot-laces together or put soot in his waistcoat-pockets. This silly and exaggerated reference to a forgotten incident of my apprentice-days angered me very much and I went in to lunch without another word. My temper had been a little frayed that morning by Matron in one of her fussy moods. She started some long rigmarole after Prayers about the boys' socks, and when I attempted to explain that the boys' socks had nothing whatever to do with me she became almost impertinent. 'Pardon me, Mr Wentworth,' she said, 'but the boys' socks have a great deal to do with *me*' (a thing I had never dreamed of denying), 'and I cannot possibly run my department properly without reasonable co-operation from the masters. What is the use of my laying out clean socks for the boys on Sunday morning if they are to be taken out for a walk in the afternoon through some of the muddiest places in Wilminster? The *state* that those boys' feet were in, Mr Wentworth! It's really too bad.' After some further inconclusive talk we parted, but the incident rankled. I am here to *teach*, not to trifle with hosiery.

I only mention this to explain why I was perhaps a little hasty with Rawlinson later in the day.

The talk about impositions recurred to me today when Mason showed up fifty lines I had had to give him for making an uncouth noise. As he handed them in immediately after break and I had only set them during the first period I asked him how he had managed to find time to do them, and he explained that he had done them in advance at the week-end. This aroused my suspicions and I looked more closely at the lines, only to find that they were not lines at all but some old history notes torn bodily from an exercise-book. Mason then said that he had done it as a protest against the system of giving lines, which he regarded as a rotten sort of impot. Naturally no self-respecting master can allow the boys to dictate to him the kind of punishment they prefer, and I told Mason pretty sharply to go to his desk and sit down; but what he had said, coupled with Rawlinson's remarks, made me wonder whether I could not devise some more satisfactory disciplinary measure.

After a little thought I hit on a plan. First I wrote down the names of the boys on a slip of paper. Then I held this up for them to see and explained that I proposed to mark a cross against the name of any boy who misbehaved in any way during the period. I should say nothing at the time, but if at the end of the period any boy had three crosses against his name he would be severely dealt with.

'What will happen?' asked Hillman.

'Wait and see, my friend,' I replied. I had not, as a matter of fact, made up my mind about this, but naturally I did not let the boys know. If there is one thing that really frightens them, it is suspense.

Clarke then asked whether a boy would only get one cross at a time, whatever he did.

'No, Clarke,' I replied. 'I shall give *two* crosses for impertinence'; and I immediately made two marks against his name on the list.

'That's not fair, sir,' he cried. 'I didn't know

we'd begun.'

I stared at him without a word until one of us was forced to look away.

'Do you want to have a *third* cross?' I asked quietly.

He made no reply, and I turned to Atkins, who had his hand up.

'May I ask a question, sir?'

'If it is a sensible one – yes,' I said, without much hope.

'I only wondered if Sapoulos gets a cross if he cries, sir.'

'Be careful, Atkins,' I warned him, taking up my pencil, and I was glad to see that there was an immediate hush. I then proceeded with the working-out of some simultaneous equations on the board, and the rest of the period passed quietly enough. Once or twice I went to my desk without a word and made an ostentatious mark on the paper, but I took care not to give any boy more than two crosses. I want more time to decide what I am going to do in cases of serious disobedience.

I was still at the board when the bell rang and several of the keener boys crowded round to ask me to explain points in the working-out that they had not understood. It was some minutes before I could get to my desk to collect my books, and when I did so I noticed at once that the punishment list had been tampered with. There were six crosses against the name of every boy except that of

Sapoulos, who had twelve. No doubt the boy who did this imagined I might not notice or that I might believe I had actually made all these marks myself. He will soon learn, whoever he is, that it is a bad mistake to underrate your enemy.

I am not going to put up with this kind of thing. Tomorrow I shall tell them that they will only have themselves to thank if I go back to the old system of lines, which they appear to dislike so much. And I shall not mince my words.

SATURDAY

The whole nib question will, I think, have to be gone into rather thoroughly at our next Common Room meeting. Would it do if the boys had a box of nibs each at the beginning of term, to be kept in their desks and used as sparingly as possible on the understanding that they had to last till the end of term? C.G. says they would get through the whole lot in a fortnight. He says they use them as ballast for paper aeroplanes and so on. I know nothing about this. I don't allow paper aeroplanes, or darts for that matter, in my classroom, and what boys do in their spare time is of course no concern of mine. But I think he exaggerates. If boys are not to be trusted to look after their own nibs the school may as well close down, it seems to me. Encourage a sense of responsibility, as the Headmaster himself says, and you are half-way to the formation of real character. I believe he would be on my side in this business. The present system wastes far too much time.

This morning I was in the middle of a rather important demonstration (tangents) on the board when Hillman asked for a new nib. I told him that he did not need a nib in order to listen to a demonstration, and he replied that he would need one as soon as they started on the Riders. 'Then ask for it then,' I said. He objected that this would mean he would lose time while the others were working and would get behindhand. I saw the justice of this, but pointed out that it would have been better for everybody if he had asked for his nib at the beginning of the period instead of interrupting the lesson half-way through. He said he had only just noticed that his nib was broken; it must have got caught in the hinge of his desk while he was looking for a ruler. I might well have asked him what business he had to be looking for a ruler when he was supposed to be following my explanation on the board, but to save time I gave him a nib from the box in my desk and told him to be more careful in future.

Three more boys then came up in quick succession and asked for nibs, and as I had given one to Hillman I could not in fairness refuse them to the others. All this delay was maddening enough, but worse was to follow, for while the third boy was standing by my desk I heard a sharp cry and looked up to see Sapoulos with his head wedged in one of the lockers, while Atkins and

Mason were trying to pull him out by the arms.
This at any rate was the explanation given me by
Mason, and I was forced to accept it, for as I
stepped down from the dais I tripped somehow
over my gown and fell to the floor, though not
heavily, so that I was unable to see whether
Sapoulos was really incapable of freeing himself or
not. By the time I had recovered my feet and
assured the boys who ran to my aid that I was
unhurt, the incident was over and the three boys
back at their desks.

Naturally I asked Sapoulos why he had gone to
his locker without permission, but he was sobbing
and unable to speak, so Atkins volunteered the
information that Sapoulos was looking, he
believed, for a pen.

I threw up my hands.

'*Where* is the boy's pen?' I demanded.

'It is in the tool-house of my gardener's aunt,'
said Mason.

I never overlook impertinence, and I gave Mason
a talking-to which he will, I think, remember as
long as he lives. I told him that he had come to
Burgrove not to be a public buffoon nor to practise
the art of being rude to those who were a good deal
older and perhaps even a little wiser than himself,
but to learn. Presumably, I said, it was the wish of
his parents who were spending their money on his
education that he should fit himself for a Public
School and afterwards for some useful career. At

present I could see no prospect of either wish being fulfilled. He would have to pull himself together and take up a very different attitude towards his school-work if he was to have the slightest chance of getting through Common Entrance; and as for a career, unless there was an unexpected demand for third-rate comedians, I could not see any way in which the world would be likely to make use of his services. 'There will have to be a big change, Mason,' I told him, 'or you and I will find ourselves at loggerheads.'

'*You* may,' he said. '*I'm* going to Cheltenham.'

I sent him out of the room at once, and when he had gone Clarke asked for some blotting-paper, which I refused. We masters always have enough nibs in our desk for the boys' needs, but pens and blotting-paper are kept in the stationery cupboard of which Rawlinson holds the key. This means that in order to gain access to the pens and so on, except at the stated times on Mondays, Wednesdays and Fridays when the cupboard is open, one has to send a chit for whatever one wants to Rawlinson. This I was not prepared to do merely to provide Clarke with blotting-paper, especially as every boy has a clean sheet put on his desk every Monday morning. Rawlinson is not particularly keen on receiving chits during morning school, and the row I had with him over the pegs in the changing-room makes me chary of asking favours. So I tore my own blotting-paper in half and gave a piece to

Clarke. He made it into a dart, which I confiscated according to my invariable rule.

We then turned our attention to the angular relationship between tangents and radii.

Mason came in while I was busy with the large wooden compasses we use for work on the board and said he was sorry if he had been rude. He said he was playing for the Second Eleven that afternoon and was rather excited. I told him I was glad to hear he had been chosen, but that he must try to remember that football was not the important thing in life. Work must come first.

This, for some reason, made all the boys laugh.

A boy called Phillips got into my bad books this afternoon. It was too wet for football after all (which was hard luck on Mason) so we all put on our macs and went for a walk, Gilbert taking the Seniors round by Fotherham Dyke, while the Juniors came with me for a ramble in Marling Woods. Sapoulos and young Hopgood asked if they might walk with me and I consented, since I like to give this privilege to all the boys in turn, and Hillman, who also asked, had the position on my right as recently as three weeks ago. I always make a note of these things; boys are so quick to notice any unfairness or favouritism.

Well, I was talking to Hopgood about footer when a boy came running back to say that Phillips was stuck in a drain and couldn't move. (I say running *back* because of course we masters always keep behind when taking a walk; it is the best place to keep an eye on the boys, see that they are wearing their caps properly and so on. The young rascals take them off and put them in their pockets if they get half a chance, which is against the School rules.)

'Phillips has no business to be in a drain at all, as you know perfectly well, Clarke,' I said brusquely; but none the less I hurried off after him as fast as I could.

We found the whole walk collected at a point where a shallow but muddy stream runs under the path through a circular drain or culvert some twelve to fifteen feet in length. I at once ordered the boys to stand away from all that mud and, pushing them aside, lowered myself cautiously to the level of the water. Then, clinging with my left hand to a convenient stump of wood, I bent down and peered into the drain. I could see nothing at all owing to the darkness, so I said, 'Come out of there at once, Phillips, d'you hear?' It had struck me immediately that he might very well be playing the fool and merely pretending to be stuck. However, there was no reply, and I repeated the order in a louder tone.

'Perhaps he'd hear better if you went round to the other end, sir,' suggested Mason, who was watching from the other side of the stream. 'His head's facing that way.'

'Just *look* at your boots, Mason!' I cried. 'Whatever will Matron say?'

I did not catch his reply, for at this moment the stump unluckily gave way and I was precipitated into the water. Instinctively I thrust out both hands as I fell, but, remembering my wrist-watch just in time, drew back my right arm without realizing that this would inevitably throw me forwards on my head. As it turned out I rolled completely over and thus failed after all to save the watch from a ducking. But by a miracle I kept my wallet dry.

'What did you say, Mason?' I asked as I rose.

'Nothing, sir.'

This I knew to be an untruth, but in the circumstances it seemed best to pass it over. Accordingly I showed my displeasure only by a look and, scrambling up the bank, made my way through a crowd of gaping boys to the other end of the culvert. Here there was no difficulty, for the bank was less steep and, my boots being already full of water, I was able to stand boldly in midstream. Almost at once I made out the white glimmer of Phillips' face just beyond a kind of iron grating which must no doubt have arrested his progress.

'Is that you, Phillips?' I asked.

'Yes, sir.'

'May I ask what you think you are doing in there?'

'I'm stuck, sir.'

'Possibly,' I said. 'Where are you stuck?'

'At the back, sir. My coat got rucked up when I tried to go back, sir, and I think – I'm not sure, sir, but I think my braces are caught on the roof, sir.'

'Are your feet wet?'

'A bit, sir.'

'Tut!' I said. 'This is a bad business, Phillips. How long have you been here?'

'About five minutes, sir.'

'Don't be ridiculous, boy!' I said angrily. 'I mean how long have you been at the School?'

'Oh, four terms, sir.'

'Quite long enough to know better,' I said sternly, and told him to stay where he was until he was released.

I then called the boys to me and told them that Phillips was caught by his braces at the back, and as his feet were wet he must be got out at once or there might be serious consequences. I explained that I was too large to enter the drain, and that one of them must therefore volunteer to crawl in at the end where – at the end which I had first investigated, and attempt to free Phillips' braces.

'Can I do it, sir?'

'Very well, Mason,' I said, 'but take off your shoes and stockings and roll up your trousers. I cannot have the whole Junior School soaking wet.'

It was an anxious time for us all while Mason was in the drain, but eventually he reappeared and clambered up the bank.

'Well, Mason?' I cried eagerly.

'I've freed his braces, sir,' he cried, holding them up.

'Mason,' I said in my coldest voice. 'This is no time for joking. Where is Phillips?'

'In the drain, sir. He daren't come out.'

Mason explained that Phillips had decided to stay in the drain because he was afraid of being punished when he came out. He said – Mason said, that is – that he thought if Phillips knew for certain nothing would happen to him he would come out at once.

'Did you suggest this to him, Mason?' I asked sternly.

'Me, sir? Good lord, no sir!'

'Tell him to come out this instant,' I cried, losing all patience with the lot of them, 'or I'll report him to the Headmaster for a thrashing.'

When Phillips came out and I saw the state of his clothes and the muddy boots of the other boys into the bargain I was in despair.

'I'd like to know what Matron will have to say about this,' I said, half to myself.

Mason, who can never learn to mind his own business, chipped in at once. 'Wouldn't it be easiest, sir,' he suggested, 'to explain that you fell into the stream and we all got a bit dirty helping you out?'

'Very easy indeed, Mason,' I replied sarcastically, 'if you can think of any reason why I *should* have fallen into the stream.'

'Need there be a special reason, sir?'

'Am I the kind of person who goes about falling into streams for no reason whatever?' I asked.

'We-ell…' said Mason.

I gave him a thundering good wigging for that piece of impertinence.

SUNDAY

'Please, sir, how do you spell "codger"?'

Among the tasks of the master on duty on Sundays is invigilation during the boys' letter-writing hour after morning chapel; though invigilation is not the right word perhaps, since one does not have to look out for cribbing or anything of that sort. One is there to help and to see that the boys keep quiet and get on with their letters. Naturally, if there was any cribbing, I mean if one boy was leaning over to see what the next boy was writing, one would put a stop to it, because they ought to be able to think of something to say to their parents on their own. Besides, we believe in the boys' correspondence being absolutely private – letters are not read and censored here or any of that nonsense, I am glad to say.

The boy who asked me to help with his spelling was young Fraser (red hair and freckles) and for a moment I failed to follow him. ' "Codger", Fraser?' I repeated. 'What sort of codger?'

'Silly old codger,' said Mason.

There was nothing to get hold of about that,

really, though I half suspected impertinence. 'Well, Fraser?' I remarked, brushing Mason's interruption aside. 'Do you particularly want to use that word? Not that there's anything against it,' I added with a smile, 'except that it's slang, of course, and rather old-fashioned slang at that.'

Some silly boy asked whether 'Geezer' would be more up to date, but I signalled to him to be quiet, and to save further argument spelled out Fraser's word. I had just returned to my book, a most interesting biography of Gustavus Adolphus, about whom I have often wondered, when another boy asked me how to spell 'coot'.

I looked up to find the whole school watching me.

'Get on, get on, you others,' I warned them. 'Are you writing nature notes, Parkinson?'

He said he was not, going rather red in the face for some reason.

'But, all the same, you wish to tell your parents something about coots, is that it?'

'Only about one, sir.'

'I see,' I said. 'A particular coot. What is there funny in that, Mason?'

'Nothing, sir.'

'Then why laugh?'

'I don't know, sir. Sir, are they really mad as well as bald, sir?'

'Stop this silly laughter immediately,' I cried, and almost at once the hubbub died down. To my surprise Mason persisted with his question, which I had not been intending to take seriously.

'Sir, why *do* people say he's as mad as a coot, sir?' he asked. 'It's an awfully funny sort of thing to say, isn't it, sir?'

'Sir, there's a book about a pig,' began Tremayne excitedly (he is not one of my IIIA boys, of course), but I cut him short. 'That will do, all of you,' I said sharply. 'Sensible questions are one thing, but we cannot spend the whole hour discussing the habits of coots. Or pigs either,' I added, with a glance at Tremayne. 'It's twenty past already.'

When Pettigrew asked me how many bats there were in 'belfry' I decided the thing was getting beyond a joke. 'No more questions for ten minutes,' I ordered. 'Any boy who is in difficulties can come up to my desk at the end of that time and ask me quietly.'

Quite a number of boys came up when the ten minutes were over, and I was explaining to de Groot about postal rates to Holland (a schoolmaster has to be an expert on a hundred and one things nowadays. Goodness knows what poor old Poole would have made of it all – he was French master here for a number of years until the boys put salt in his hair. There were one or two other contretemps as a matter of fact; the Headmaster might have overlooked an isolated incident). Well, I was talking to de Groot, as I was saying, when an infernal shindy broke out about half-way down the queue.

'Stop that scrimmaging about there,' I shouted. 'Fraser, what are you doing?'

'Somebody hacked me on the heel, sir.'

'Sneak,' said Mason.

'It isn't sneaking to say "somebody".'

'Oh, no! Considering nobody could have hacked you except the next man in the queue.'

'You're sneaking yourself now,' said Fraser.

I put my spectacles down firmly on the desk and rose to my feet.

'Go to your desks all of you,' I said quietly. 'I will not have this ridiculous arguing and bickering during Letter-Hour. You can all just get on with it straight away without any more fuss. And *stop* fiddling with that watch, Jenkins. You've written practically nothing.'

Jenkins is a new boy, who probably hasn't had a watch of his own before, but all the same he has been here long enough now to know that he must not fiddle with it in class, or in Letter-Hour, which comes to the same thing. He told me, feebly, that he didn't know what to say.

'My dear boy,' I replied. 'Surely you can write your own letters home. This is not supposed to be Dictation period. Tell them what you did last week. Tell them what is going to happen next week, if you like.'

'*Is* anything going to happen next week?' asked Mason.

I always try to avoid sarcasm, but this was too much. 'Considering the School plays Fox House away on Wednesday and on Thursday there is a lecture on the Ice Age – '

'With slides?' asked some fool.

' – and the second monthly form-order will be out at the weekend, even you, Mason,' I continued smoothly, 'can hardly regard next week as a complete blank. What boy interrupted me just now?'

Nobody owned up, so I put on a Silence rule. 'Anybody who speaks in this room without my permission,' I told them, 'will get a hundred lines.' You could have heard a pin drop. I did hear a nib, as a matter of fact – Mason of course. But I had my eye on him, and he bent down and picked it up without a word. Then, as ill-luck would have it, Miss Coombes came in with some music lists.

'Oh, Mr Wentworth,' she began, but the rest of the sentence was lost in a gale of laughter in which, I am ashamed to say, I could not refrain from joining. Somehow the idea of coming down on poor Miss Coombes with a hefty impot was irresistibly comic.

She went very red in the face and marched out without another word, not understanding the joke, of course. I am afraid she will be upset, though I shall make a point of explaining things to her after lunch, naturally.

The absurd incident had one good effect, for the

boys settled down straight away, everybody scribbling away quite contentedly for the rest of the hour. I had my suspicions of what they were all writing about – suspicions which were pretty well confirmed when, right at the end, Fraser asked me how to spell embarrassed.

'Two "r's", Fraser,' I told him, and was unable to resist adding, 'The "ass", no doubt you are familiar with?'

The boys were quick to appreciate my little dig at him and everybody laughed. They laughed still more when Fraser replied, 'Yes, thank you, sir. I've got him down already,' though I confess I failed to see the point.

Anyway, I hope they won't say anything derogatory about Miss Coombes in their letters. She is a friendly soul, though inclined to be a little weak – of which the boys, I have reason to think, sometimes take advantage.

Lent Term 1939
The Man Faggott

After the bustle and excitement of the first day of term it was a real shock to me to be informed quite casually by Gilbert this morning that he is taking over eleven o'clock milkers. Eleven o'clock milkers is our name here for the distribution of milk during break to certain boys whose parents have expressed a wish that they should have it, and for years it has been my prerogative to tick off the names of these boys as they come up for their glasses. The last thought in my mind as I entered the Common Room after breakfast was that any change could be contemplated in this arrangement – certainly not without consulting me.

Of course I went straight off to the Headmaster the moment I heard of it.

I found him interviewing some parents who had brought their boy, a new boy, down a day late, and would have withdrawn at once, but Mr Saunders beckoned me in.

'Ah, Wentworth!' he cried, 'I'm glad you looked in. Mr Wentworth is one of our little community of assistant masters, Mrs Carter – a very happy little community, eh, Wentworth? I'm sure he will help Johnny all he can.'

'How do you do, Mrs Carter?' I said. 'We will certainly do our best to put young Johnny on the right road. You need have no doubt that he will be happy here at Burgrove – and work hard, won't you, Johnny?'

The little boy made no reply, and I turned to his father.

'Why, Mr Carter,' I exclaimed admiringly, 'he's the living image of you!'

'I should have introduced you,' put in Mrs Carter, colouring prettily. 'This is Captain Ferguson, a very kind friend who motored us down.'

It would have been the work of a moment to cover up this little misunderstanding, but in stepping backwards to address a remark about the mild weather to Mrs Carter I had the misfortune to tread on her boy's foot; he had somehow got round behind me in that irritating way young people have. Naturally I apologized, but he burst into tears, and indeed made a most unnecessary fuss about the incident.

'Come, come, Johnny,' I said kindly. 'You are a big boy now. You must learn to put up with a few hard knocks now you have come to Burgrove.'

'Why is that, Mr Wentworth?' cried his mother,

mistaking my meaning. 'Do you make a point of treading on the boys' feet at this school?'

'No, Mrs Carter,' I replied, turning the point neatly, though perfectly politely, against her. 'We teach the boys to stand on their *own* feet at Burgrove.'

'Well, Wentworth,' said the Headmaster, rather shortly for him, 'is there anything you want to see me about?'

'Nothing that will not keep until you are free, thank you, Headmaster,' I replied, and with a smile that included them all I turned on my heel and walked into a maidenhair fern which Mr Saunders, rashly as I think, keeps on a tall stand by the door. Only great quickness on my part saved the pot from falling to the floor, and finding myself with the fern in my arms I decided that the best thing to do was to walk straight out with it, pretending that I had meant all along to take it with me. This naturally made it impossible for me to shut the door, and thus as I walked through the swing-door into the boys' part of the house I overheard Mrs Carter make a remark which I greatly resented. Nothing is to be gained by repeating it here.

I had a busy day and had almost forgotten the trifling annoyances of the morning, when the Headmaster summoned me to his study.

'Well, Wentworth,' he began, 'have you any explanation to offer?'

'Explanation?' I stammered.

'Of your rudeness to one of our parents and your extraordinary action in removing an ornament from my room without permission and without explanation of any kind?'

'If you are referring to the maidenhair fern,' I replied, controlling myself with difficulty, 'I can only say that I should have thought my reasons for taking it were obvious.'

'Not to me,' he said, and added that even if he could conceive some object for which a fern was necessary in my day's work, as for example to illustrate some scientific point to the boys or as a drawing model – though it would be news to him to learn that I was concerned with the teaching either of science or drawing at Burgrove, even so he still could not imagine that the need was of such urgency as to justify the methods I had adopted to acquire one. He had heard, he went on, of men subject to sudden ungovernable impulses which made the possession of some desired object a paramount consideration, but if that was the explanation he only wished I had given him some inkling of my desire for a maidenhair fern. He could then have had one placed in my room at the beginning of term and this deplorable incident would have been avoided. But on the whole, he said, he preferred to think that my action was simply a particularly mistaken and ill-timed piece of clowning.

'If that is what you think, Headmaster,' I burst

out at last, 'I have no option but to resign my position here. I have spent many happy, and I like to think not unproductive, years at Burgrove, and I shall be sorry, more than sorry, to go –

'We shall be sorry to lose you, Wentworth.'

'There is no reason why you *should* lose me,' I rejoined warmly. 'The whole ridiculous incident has been magnified out of all proportion. I will go and fetch this precious fern *now*. That I should be accused at my age of kleptomania and – and clownishness – is incredible!'

Blind with rage I turned to the door, but as ill luck would have it, caught my foot against the fern-stand and went down heavily against a table of silver spoons and other small bric-à-brac. When I rose to my feet, still automatically clutching the stand, there were tears of mortification in my eyes.

'Headmaster –' I began.

'Leave me the stand, Wentworth,' he cried, 'at least leave me the stand!' and to my amazement I saw that he was smiling.

I would have spoken, but he checked me with a gesture.

'Never mind about it now,' he said. 'We'll talk about it later. And let me have my fern back when you've finished with it, won't you?'

I said good night, and as I walked away an explosion of laughter followed me down the corridor. I went to my room to write up this diary with my mind in a whirl.

WEDNESDAY, 1 FEBRUARY

[The following account of an incident, not mentioned in Mr Wentworth's diary, has been sent to me by Mr Charles Gilbert, one of his colleagues. It sheds a certain light on some of the pitfalls of the profession.]

I hear that old ass Wentworth has been sending you extracts from his precious diary, though what he hopes to gain by it goodness only knows. But I don't suppose for a moment he has made any mention of the great Night Alarm – one of his finest exploits, and I thought you might like to know about it.

Well, one night I was sitting in my room down at the Masters' Cottage taking my boots off and fearing no evil, when I heard a great disturbance next door, and in a moment Wentworth came tearing in with an incoherent story about not being able to get into bed and how he'd make trouble for Mrs Barnett over this in the morning. I went along with him to investigate and, as I'd rather expected, found he'd got an apple-pie bed. As I say, I wasn't surprised because as a matter of fact I'd made it myself, but what did astonish me was that Wentworth obviously didn't know what it was. That's the trouble with him. You never can gauge the depths of the man's simplicity. He seemed to think that Mrs Barnett, who does for us at the cottage, had made a hash of her job when she made up the bed, and he was absolutely set on putting her through it for what he called her 'abominable

carelessness'. Naturally I didn't want Mrs Barnett
to be unjustly accused, so I explained that sometimes people went into other people's rooms and
turned up the bottom sheet in this way simply in
order to surprise the owner of the room when he
went to bed. 'Just as a joke,' I added.

'But who could have done such a senseless
thing?' he asked.

He looked quite upset about it, so I shook my
head. But I thought there was no harm in
mentioning that I'd seen Collingridge hanging
about the cottage just after dinner.

'Collingridge!' said Wentworth. 'I thought he
had more sense.' You could see the idea came as
quite a shock to him, but after a while I persuaded
him that the only way to settle it was to go straight
up to Collingridge's room and tax him with it.
'Pull the bedclothes off him, A.J.,' I said. 'Then
he'll leave you alone in future.'

In the end he put some clothes on and set off.
Collingridge sleeps up at the school, because
there's no room in the cottage, and my idea was
that he'd just about have had time to clear out the
holly I'd put in his bed and get settled down for
the night before Wentworth arrived. Then if
Wentworth took my advice and whipped the
clothes off him I thought there might possibly be
some fun...

The last thing I expected to hear was the fire-
alarm going.

What happened apparently was this. Wentworth, with his peculiar genius for taking the wrong turning and a good deal aided by the fact that all the lights in the school corridors are switched off at half-past ten, went slap into Matron's room, which lies relatively in the same position on the right at the top of the main stairs as Collingridge's room does on the left. He got out again, he says, before she got to the light-switch, but her screams must have upset him because he ran too much to the right and came a most frightful purler over a row of enamel water-jugs they put out along the wall of the corridor ready for the morning. Well, you know the kind of noise a lot of empty enamelware makes when you start it rolling about the floor and down the stairs. Wentworth, I should imagine, lost his nerve altogether, and it must have been more luck than judgement that made him bolt into Collingridge's room.

Collingridge, who had had about enough of all this disturbance, hit him a tremendous wallop with a pillow just as Matron set the fire-alarm going.

I'm told there was a fair amount of pandemonium. The rule is that on hearing the alarm at night all boys are to put on their dressing-gowns and proceed in an orderly manner to the gymnasium – unless, I suppose, the gymnasium happens to be on fire; but I don't believe there's any provision for that. All I know is that when I got to the gym everybody seemed to be talking at once, and in the middle of it Matron was trying to explain to the Headmaster, who looks a good deal less impressive in a check dressing-gown, that there wasn't any fire but that somebody, or so she thought – though she might have been mistaken – had attempted to get into her bedroom. ('Get back to your dormitories, all you boys,' said the Reverend Saunders at this point.) Anyway, what *had* alarmed her and made her feel it was her duty, to the boys if not to herself, to ring the alarm, was a terrible noise as if some kind of wild beast were crashing and rolling about among the hot-water jugs in the corridor.

The moment old Saunders heard this about the jugs he began to look round for Wentworth. The fact is that whenever you hear a loud crash at Burgrove or see a pile of play-boxes or bowler-hats toppling to the ground you instinctively expect to catch sight of Wentworth making an unobtrusive disappearance round a corner, and you are very rarely disappointed. Wentworth wasn't in the gym, as he should have been after a fire-alarm, and I thought it only right to point out that Collingridge wasn't there either. 'No doubt,' I said, 'there is some perfectly good reason for their absence.'

There was. It became painfully clear, to me at least, what was detaining them as soon as we reached the top of the main stairs, but to the others I dare say the thudding sounds that came from the direction of Collingridge's room only made the mystery more mysterious.

'Odd!' said the Headmaster, pausing. 'Very odd. Do you think I should go in?'

For myself, I thought it far better that he shouldn't, but on the spur of the moment I could think of no argument to support this view. So I nodded dumbly and followed him in.

What old Saunders expected to see I have no idea, but I am pretty certain that it never struck him he might be intruding on a death-grapple between two of his assistant masters. The room was a shambles, but it was the combatants who took the eye. At the moment of our entry they had got themselves into a corner beyond the bed, where Collingridge, with his head in Wentworth's stomach, was trying with a conscientiousness one could not help admiring to thrust him into a cupboard obviously two or three sizes too small for him. Wentworth, a good deal handicapped by having a sheet over his head and both feet practically off the ground, was contenting himself with belabouring his opponent's back with his fists, but I must say he was making a sound job of it.

'*Get* in there, can't you?' Collingridge was saying, butting hard.

'Ouch!' said Wentworth.

'*Wentworth*!' cried the Headmaster in an awful voice. 'Are you mad?'

The question that so many have asked themselves at various stages of Wentworth's career might have been answered then and there if only the old boy hadn't been too short of wind and too much bothered by the sheet to reply. While they were getting themselves disentangled and Wentworth was doing his bashful utmost to scrape the cupboard off his back, I took my leave. I thought that they could probably explain the whole thing between them without any help from me.

But, as I told Wentworth next morning, he'll really have to learn to control his passions a bit better or he'll be getting the sack. Of course I was referring to his scrap with Collingridge, but for some reason of his own he chose to think I meant the Matron. You never saw a man in such a lather. [*This concludes Mr Gilbert's narrative.*]

TUESDAY, 14 FEBRUARY

People ask me sometimes whether I find the schoolboy of today noticeably quieter and more mature than his elder brother of, say, the early thirties. I cannot see it. I detect precious little difference in the young rascals. More knowledgeable perhaps on some subjects, aircraft modelling to take an obvious instance, but as bone-headed as ever over the important things. I can still twist their tails with a simultaneous quadratic; and it is still just as difficult to make them see that unless they stick to a problem, really worry at it, for themselves, instead of throwing up their hands and shouting 'Sir, Sir,' at the slightest set-back, they will never make mathematicians.

And the *time* we waste. Yesterday, after break, I told Set IIIA to write down one third as a decimal.

'Everybody finished?' I asked.

'No, sir,' said Mason.

I gave him another half-minute and then told him to stop.

'But it *won't* stop, sir.'

Everybody laughed.

'I mean it goes on and on, sir, and if I stop before it does my answer won't be right.'

'What have you got, Mason?'

'Well, sir, so far I've got point three three three three three three three three three three three three three three three three – that's correct to sixteen decimal places, sir.'

'There's nothing to laugh about!' I said sharply. 'What have you got there, Atkins?'

'Me, sir? Point three recurring, sir.'

'I am not asking for the answer to the sum. I am asking you what you have got in your right hand.'

'Nothing, sir.'

Boys invariably try this answer first, though they must know they have precious little chance of getting away with it with an old hand like me. Atkins had that boiled look that tells you at once when a boy is caught out.

'Bring it up here, Atkins,' I said. 'And the rest of you express point seven three five as a fraction.'

I wrote it up on the board to stop endless

questions and then took the piece of paper Atkins handed to me.

He had simply scribbled the Headmaster's name, 'Rev. Gregory Saunders, MA', on the paper, and I was about to send him back to his desk with a caution against wasting the time of the form when I noticed that the paper was folded over at the bottom.

'An old dodge, Atkins,' I said, unfolding it.

He had written 'The Beast of Burgrove' under the Headmaster's name, a serious offence.

'I can't possibly overlook this, Atkins,' I told him sternly.

'Couldn't you overlook it on his birthday, sir?' asked Mason.

'Is it your birthday, Atkins?' I asked.

'No, sir.'

'In that case, Mason, I fail to see the point of your remark. Even if it was any business of yours – '

'I was only wondering, sir, whether if it *had* been his birthday, it would have made any difference.'

'Mason!' I warned him. 'That will do. When I want your advice about the way to treat people on their birthday, I will ask for it. Birthdays make no difference to the fact that we've all come here to work, and the sooner everyone realizes that the better.'

'Is it your birthday, sir?' somebody called out, and there was an immediate chorus of cries from the other boys. 'Jolly good, Duce,' 'Wake up,

Duce,' 'Have some macaroni, Benito,' and a lot more nonsense of the same kind, which I very soon stamped on. Benito is not the boy's real name, of course (though we have quite a number of French and Belgians here now, besides Sapoulos, the Greek; and a little Dutch boy called de Groot came last term); but the others call him that because of some fancied resemblance to the Italian leader.

'Now then,' I said. 'Let's see who's got this fraction right. Otterway?'

'Not quite ready yet, sir.'

'Hurry up, boy. Trench?'

'Well, sir, I've done it, only it seems rather an absurd answer.

'Never mind that,' I said. 'I'm used to absurd answers. What is it?'

'A hundred and forty-seven over two hundred.'

'What's absurd about that? Well, Williamson?'

'I thought I heard the bell, sir.'

I slammed my book down on the desk.

'If you would kindly attend to your work, instead of listening for the school bell, we might conceivably get through a fraction of what we have to do before the end of term – perhaps even a hundred and forty-seven two hundredths of it, Trench.'

'Jolly good, sir!' said Mason.

I told them they might go, and began to collect my things for my English period.

'May I go too, sir?' asked Atkins, about whom, I

am bound to confess, I had rather forgotten.

I took up a piece of chalk and tossed it in the air.

'What are we going to do about this, Atkins?' I said. 'Eh?'

'I don't know, sir. I'm sorry, sir.'

'H'm!' I said, not knowing either. 'I'll have to think about it.'

I shall probably decide to do nothing in the end. The boy has had a good fright, which is the main thing.

WEDNESDAY, 1 MARCH

Rawlinson is down with flu and a man called Faggott has come in for a week or two. He is a Major apparently – one of those stocky red-faced men with a moustache which sprouts out in a disagreeable way over uneven yellow teeth. He whistles too, and is – well, more abrupt in manner towards some of the regular staff than one altogether expects or relishes. No doubt it is difficult to get the right type of man for such a short appointment, but still – there are agencies and so on which cater for this kind of emergency. One wonders if he has had much experience really; and I'm bound to say the one place one does hear of his having been at doesn't seem to me to be quite – though it's easy enough to get a false impression of these things. 'Not the way we used to do things at Marston House' – if he's said that once in the last three days he's said it a hundred times. As if we cared how they choose to do things at some potty little seaside school or other. 'All I can say is,' I remarked at last, goaded beyond endurance by some petty criticism of one of our school rules – he had chosen to be offensive, if I remember rightly, because the boys here line up in their school order when the bell rings for meals and march to their places in an orderly fashion (a thoroughly wise arrangement, as it happens) – 'All I can say is,' I remarked, 'if that's not the way you used to do it at Marston House, so much the worse for Marston House'; and I walked straight in to my place at Gainsborough (each table in the dining-room is known by the name of a famous artist or soldier – another old custom that Faggott has not hesitated to make the subject of his stupid pleasantries) without giving him a chance to reply. I was thoroughly angry.

Then this morning I told him in a perfectly friendly way that the Headmaster did not expect to see masters smoking in the school corridors or classrooms, though of course it was quite all right in Common Room. 'Rats to that!' he said, and strolled off down the passage with his foul, stumpy little pipe clamped firmly between his teeth. What can one do with such a fellow?

It is worse down at the Cottage. This evening he came barging into my room with a bottle of whisky in his hand looking for soda. 'This chap Rawlinson doesn't seem to have any in his room,' he said.

Rawlinson is in the San, so Faggott has been given his room. It was on the tip of my tongue to say that Rawlinson had probably locked up his soda, and would, no doubt, if he had known who was to take his place, have locked up his whisky as well; but instead I merely replied that I had no soda to offer him and went quietly on with my correction of IIIA's work. I had a great deal to do and my manner ought to have made it clear to anyone that I was busy and wished to be left alone. But a nod is as good as a wink to a blind horse. Major Faggott wandered about the room, whistling between his teeth, examining my belongings in the coolest possible fashion, picking up a book here and a book there and laying it down again with a groan, pausing with sharp exclamations of disgust in front of my Van Gogh reproductions and my college groups, going so far even as to take up a photograph of my sister from the mantelpiece and replace it without comment behind the ormolu clock.

'Well,' I said at last when I could stand it no longer, 'you don't appear to have much work to do.'

He came and leaned over my shoulder. ''Ullo, 'ullo!' he said, draggling his pipe-stem over the papers. 'Those curly brackets ought to have been taken out, or I'm a Dutchman. Three out of five.'

'Are you a mathematician, Major Faggott?'

'Me!' he said. 'You've heard of the Binomial Theorem?'

'I should hope so,' I said stiffly.

'Well, I invented it.'

'Indeed!' I said, making no attempt to keep the contempt out of my voice. 'I was under the impression that it was invented by Omar Khayyám.'

He roared with laughter. 'What a queer old buffer it is! Haven't you ever read the *Rubaiyat*?'

'I have,' I answered. 'I have also read *Alice in Wonderland*. It is quite possible for a man to be a writer as well as a mathematician – just as it should be possible for a man to be a gentleman as well as a schoolmaster.'

'It isn't,' he said, quite failing to see the implication of my remark; 'that's why I've practically given up schoolmastering.'

I made no reply, contenting myself with ostentatiously marking my papers, and there was silence for a long time, so that I began to hope the man had gone. But when at last I turned round in my chair I saw him still fiddling with the things on my mantelpiece.

'No photograph of the Matron, I see,' he said with an unpleasant grin.

I rose to my feet and demanded to know what he meant by that remark. He then made a suggestion so offensive that for a moment I was unable to speak, while the hot blood mounted to my cheeks. Never in all my years at Burgrove have I been spoken to in such a way – and by such a preposterous bounder. It is typical of the man that he misinterpreted my natural flush of indignation and was pleased to describe it as a 'guilty blush'. I believe I might have struck him where he stood, but fortunately he saw that I was in a dangerous mood and decided to take his leave.

'Well,' he said with an attempt at nonchalance, 'if you've no soda in this rat-trap I may as well be pushing along,' and he swaggered off, turning a photograph of my old College Eight to the wall as he went out.

I went straight along to Gilbert's room as soon as he had gone. The fact is that that reference of Faggott's to a silly incident of a few weeks ago was the last straw. The whole thing was too childish. I simply tripped up in the dark one night when I was on my way to ask Collingridge about something or other, and Matron, whose room is not far away, was frightened by the noise and rang the fire-alarm. Some silly fool has exaggerated the story and told it to this impossible Faggott, who is not above twisting the whole thing round to suit his own purposes and make me look ridiculous, or worse. So I have put the whole position before Gilbert and he agrees that something must be done to put the Major – if he is a Major, which I begin to doubt – in his place. We have a sort of a plan which we think may make it clear to the Headmaster that Faggott is not at all the type for a school of this sort. Better have nobody at all until Rawlinson comes back, as I said to Gilbert, than allow a mischief-maker like Faggott the run of the place for another fortnight. I could take Rawlinson's lot with my own, if it comes to that. The desks from both classrooms would have to be moved into the gym, I suppose, though that might interfere with the Sergeant's fencing-classes. Still, fencing isn't everything.

Gilbert approved of my gym plan when I told him of it and suggested I might invigilate from the vaulting-horse – but I don't think he was serious.

MONDAY, 6 MARCH

The man Faggott continues to be a thorn in my side. Naturally as the next senior master I expected to be put in charge of the stationery cupboard during Rawlinson's absence; but Faggott, so he says, was definitely instructed by the Headmaster when he took up his temporary position here to perform all Rawlinson's duties as far as possible, and it is typical of the man's dog-in-the-manger attitude that he insists on interpreting the phrase to cover the supervision of stationery, despite his obvious lack of experience at work of this kind. This morning being Monday the cupboard was open from 9.0 to 9.30, and I thought it best to keep an eye on Faggott while the boys were coming up in turn for their requirements. As I expected, it was not long before I saw him handing out some of the special pink blotting-paper which is kept for Common Room use.

I thought it my duty to step forward and put him right at once, though I was careful to speak in a low voice in order not to discredit him in front of the boys.

'White blotting-paper?' he said, affecting to misunderstand me, and he handed me a couple of sheets without troubling to turn round.

'I do not, require blotting-paper, thank you,' I said curtly.

'You soak it up yourself, eh?' he replied, accompanying this meaningless remark with a wink which made my temper rise at once. But in view of the presence of a number of boys I controlled myself and merely said it was good news to hear Rawlinson would be up again in a day or two. I think he knew what I meant.

After this it was particularly galling to hear his praises sung so loudly by IIIA during the first period after break. Apparently he has been currying favour with the boys by means of a certain facility he has for mechanical repairs, and also (and less surprisingly to those who know him) by boasting of his exploits in the Great War. Boys are extraordinarily easily taken in by men of his – I had almost said 'flashy' – type. As a result I was obliged to listen to a long account from Atkins of how Faggott had tunnelled his way out of a German fortress with a penknife, or some such nonsense, and when that was over Mason showed me a watch he had mended, and Hillman brought up a mechanical crane which had been newly soldered – not too well, in my opinion, though I am no artisan – just above the base. I told Hillman, rather abruptly, for I was getting tired of all this, that the classroom was no place for cranes, and a voice immediately said, 'Or pigeons' – an impertinent reference, or so I took it, to an occasion last term when a pigeon mysteriously flew out of my desk.

'Stand up the boy who said that!' I cried, and to my surprise the whole class rose to their feet. However, I am too old a hand not to recognize a concerted attempt at ragging when I see it, and I promptly decided to play them at their own game and beat them at it.

'You all said it?' I asked, only slightly raising my eyebrows. 'Very well, then, you will all be punished. A hundred lines each by tomorrow morning.'

There was a chorus of 'Oh, sir!'s which I immediately suppressed by a threat to double the imposition, and Mason then asked whether Sapoulos had to do the lines as well. I had failed to notice that the little Greek boy had remained sitting while the others got up, and my suspicions were immediately aroused.

'Did you say it, Sapoulos?' I asked sternly.

'I beg to be excused, sir,' he replied.

There was a general laugh at his quaint English, but knowing that he meant to say, 'I beg your pardon?' I repeated my question: 'Did you say "Or pigeons"?'

' "Orpigeons", sir?'

'You heard what I said.'

Sapoulos, instead of replying, kept repeating 'orpigeons, orpigeons, orpigeons' over to himself in a puzzled tone until I lost all patience with the boy.

'Sapoulos!' I thundered, 'did you or did you not say "Or pigeons"?'

The silly boy, as I feared, now began to cry, and Mason volunteered the opinion that he probably thought 'or pigeons' was one word and didn't know what it meant. I told him that when I wanted his advice I would ask for it, and added that as nearly half the period had already been wasted we should not do mental arithmetic, as I had promised, but instead would refresh our memories of Pythagoras. 'And stop that groaning,' I added sharply.

I had barely completed the construction on the blackboard when some boy – Mason again, I think – calmly announced, without even troubling to hold up his hand: 'Major Faggott says there's a much easier way of proving it than that – by trigonometry or something.'

I walked to my desk and carefully balanced my chalk on the ledge. 'Is Major Faggott teaching you geometry,' I asked, striving to keep my voice under control, 'or am I?'

'Neither,' said Mason under his breath – but not quietly enough to save the whole set from being kept in for an hour this afternoon.

I attribute the indiscipline with which I had to deal this morning entirely to the influence of Faggott. When one of the staff, however temporary, swaggers about the place setting rules at naught, ridiculing the school customs, smoking in the corridors and (as I actually heard at lunch today) openly admitting his intention of running up to Town to see one of the most *risqué* musical-comedies of the day, how can one expect the boys to remain uncontaminated? The last straw, to me personally, came this afternoon when in the hearing of several quite junior boys, including one new boy, he loudly addressed me as 'The Great Wen' – a punning allusion, presumably, to the first syllable of my name. If it were not for an instinctive dislike of anything that savours of sneaking I should long ago have gone to the Headmaster. That I shall do only as a last resort. Meanwhile, as Gilbert says, there are other ways....

THURSDAY, 9 MARCH

Boys are curious creatures. This morning, apropos of some point that arose in connexion with percentages, Williamson asked whether it was true that schoolmasters were to be exempt from National Service, and I said I believed it was and explained that even in wartime education had to go on. Several boys said it was a swizz (meaning

swizzle). Hopgood II then advanced the extraordinary theory that in an emergency everybody
who had a moustache would be compelled to shave
it off. If Mason or Atkins had made such a statement
I should come down on them pretty sharply, as I
wear a small moustache myself and have had reason
in the past to suspect both these boys of impertinence (though, to be fair, not actually on that
subject), but Hopgood II is a quiet studious boy,
who, as I wrote in his Report last term, is keen on his
work and should do well. So I asked him, with a
smile, what would be the purpose of such an
extreme measure, to which he replied that he
thought it had something to do with mustard gas
and that people with moustaches would be more
difficult to decontaminate than those without. This
made Mason and some of the others laugh so
immoderately that I had to call the set to order.

'That will do,' I said sharply. 'Stranger things
than that may happen in war.'

Etheridge suddenly shouted out 'Beards !' and
went very red when I asked him to explain himself.
He apologized and said he had just realized that
Hopgood must mean beards, not moustaches,
because you couldn't get a gas-mask on with a
beard because it had to be rolled up inside and then
it choked you, or anyway you couldn't see clearly
through the eyepieces.

'That is as it may be, Etheridge,' I began, 'but we
are not here to discuss whether or not beards can

be worn with gas-masks –'

'Couldn't they cut a slit in the chin part to let the beard out?' interrupted Mason rather rudely.

'Say "Sir" if you are speaking to me, Mason,' I reminded him, but it turned out that he was speaking to Etheridge.

I hoped that this not very edifying discussion was now at an end, but Williamson, despite a warning frown from me, started an argument with Mason about the effects of mustard gas on beards, objecting that if a beard was left hanging outside the mask it would be destroyed. Mason said he didn't believe it and anyway it wouldn't matter much if it was, and Hillman then chipped in with the remark that it was a pity old Mr Poole (our dear old French master, who retired a year ago) wasn't still here; they could have put some mustard on his beard and watched the result.

'He put a good deal on it himself in his time,' Mason said, 'and nothing happened.'

'It grew longer, if anything,' said Atkins.

One of the things every schoolmaster has to learn sooner or later is never to permit, still less to encourage, criticism of his colleagues. Nothing is more fatal to discipline than to appear even for a moment to countenance any lack of respect for another master, whatever one's personal opinions may be (it went against the grain, for instance, to punish Otterway the other day for a remark he made about Major Faggott, but I had to do it); and

I certainly did not propose to allow a slighting reference to such a faithful old friend and loyal servant of the school as Mr Poole, just because he was no longer with us. I told them pretty straight that it was cowardly to attack people behind their backs, and I was not going to have it; they would never have dared to suggest putting mustard on Mr Poole's beard if he had been still at Burgrove.

I had forgotten, as a matter of fact, until Mason reminded me of it, that they did actually put salt in the old man's hair one day towards the end of his time here, when he was losing something of his vigour and grip. How it was done remains a mystery. According to one story the salt was sprinkled in his hat; according to another they somehow persuaded poor Poole that it was good for his scalp and put it on with his consent. Yet a third account says that it was not ordinary salt but effervescent, and that the point of the joke (if such it could be called) came when he smoothed down his hair, as was his invariable custom, with a damp brush. But whatever the truth of the matter, it was a cruel prank and nothing, as I told Mason, to laugh about.

'However,' I went on, 'as you all seem so interested in the subject of gas-masks, let me see what you can make of this: In a town of four thousand five hundred inhabitants two hundred and forty of the men were bearded...'

'In Greece,' remarked Sapoulos, 'that would

give surprise.'

'How many of the women?' asked Atkins.

I mention these stupid interjections only to observe that a schoolmaster's success or failure in dealing with young boys depends upon the extent to which he allows himself to be disconcerted or thrown out of his stride by over-eager or ill-timed interruptions. Experience has taught me that to ignore them is often quite sufficient rebuke to the boys concerned. Spoken reproof, except in cases of glaring impertinence or insubordination, is unnecessary and may lead to endless controversy. The golden rule is: Never allow oneself to be side-tracked.

'– what percentage of the population,' I proceeded smoothly, 'would find an ordinary gas-mask difficult or impossible to adjust?'

One or two boys, as usual, wanted the question repeated, but in two or three minutes they were all hard at work. Nothing arouses their keenness so much as a really practical problem to solve, and of course there was the added incentive of ten marks for the first boy to show up the correct answer, nine for the second, and so on. I had hardly had time to jot down the figures myself before Etheridge arrived at my desk to claim the highest mark, followed in quick succession by Hillman, Trench and Williamson. Then Anderson and Atkins had a race, though they know perfectly well that I will not have running or scrapping in the classroom, and ended by knocking over my ink-pot. I whipped open the desk, through the hinge of which the ink was already beginning to pour, and to my dismay found that I had only a small scrap of blotting-paper. The boys helped with what they had, but it was quite insufficient to deal with the situation. There was nothing for it but to send Etheridge off with a note to Major Faggott, who has taken over Rawlinson's duties in charge of the stationery commissariat – loth though I was to ask any favour of the man. I took care to explain the urgency of the case, and so could hardly believe my eyes when Etheridge returned without any blotting-paper but with a brief *unsealed* note from Faggott saying 'Soak it up yourself'.

I put the note in my pocket without a word and went straight along to Faggott's classroom. I found him with his feet up on the desk, reading to the boys, I was quick to notice, from Green's *History of the English People*, though I know for a fact that Rawlinson uses Oman. 'Hallo!' he said, not troubling to alter his position. 'Anything wrong?'

I was boiling with rage but controlled myself in front of the form and simply said that I was sorry to disturb him in any way (with a meaning glance at his feet, but I must have blotting-paper at once, as there had been an accident.

'Well,' he said, 'the cupboard's open.'

I turned on my heel and left the room. It was quite obvious that it never entered his head to come along with me and hand out the blotting-paper himself in the proper manner. Not that I minded fetching it myself, in a way, but that the stationery cupboard should be left like that, *unlocked* on a *Thursday*....

I shall not, of course, allow the matter to rest there.

SUNDAY, 12 MARCH

[*The following entries appear to have been made at different times on the same day: the first, I should say, just before supper, the second, which is not always easy to read and in places, to tell the truth, is downright illegible, later on in the evening.*]

Faggott's last day. He goes, I believe, early tomorrow morning, and I for one shall not be sorry to see the last of him. One learns as a schoolmaster to rub along with all sorts and conditions of men – 'Look for the good qualities not the bad in your colleagues' is a useful motto, generally speaking, for Common Room life – but really, for anyone who cares for the good name of the school and who feels, well, without any snobbishness, that the teaching of young boys is a job better left to gentlemen (in the best sense of the word, of course), I must say that the last fortnight or so has been something of a trial. However, least said, perhaps, soonest mended.

In view of all that has happened I was thunderstruck, to say the least, when Gilbert told me quite casually this afternoon that Faggott proposed to hold a farewell party in his room after supper and hoped I would come along. I thought it typical of the man's monstrous cheek and said so; wild horses, I told him would not drag me to any party of Faggott's – even one which was to cele-brate his departure. But Gilbert was most persuasive. After all, he said, the man was going and what was the use of bearing a grudge? 'Besides,' he added with a wink, 'I happen to know that Faggott is going to see the Squid at half-past ten tonight.'

'Steady!' I said, glancing anxiously round to see if any of the boys had heard the disrespectful term. 'They'll be out of the boot-room in a moment. Anyway, what has Faggott's interview with the Headmaster got to do with it?'

'Well,' Gilbert said, 'it has occurred to me that if it's pretty obvious, even to the Reverend Saunders, that Faggott has been celebrating when he goes to see him, there won't be much risk of Faggott getting asked here again, if you see what I mean. You don't want him back, do you? Very well, then, that's why I want you to come. The more there are of us, the merrier he will be. See the point?'

I confess I did not altogether care for Gilbert's suggestion, even if, as I half suspect, he only meant it in fun, but remembering what he had said about not bearing a grudge and so on, I consented to look in at Faggott's party for a few moments. It is to be at eight o'clock, apparently. Supper is at seven here on Sundays.

The Headmaster was bitterly resentful of his attitude. Bitterly. Look at my trousers. My coat and trousers are not what they were not what they were. What will Matron say when she sees my trousers and my coat and trousers? Trousers trousers trousers trousers trowsers? trews rather. *Bracæ*=trews. What will Matron say? It is no business of hers. None at all. My trousers are my own pigeon as I told the Headmaster. I regret his attitude and I told him. Bitterly.

'WHO PUT THAT PIGEON IN MY TROUSERS?'

Never mind the pigeon now, Wentworth, Esq., BA. Let me tell the story in my own way. I went to Faggott's room and Collingridge and Gilbert and Rawlinson has been ill but there he was. I am Senior Mathmatics master at Burgrove Preparatory School and I went to Faggott's room. Mathmatics mathematics. Who put the 'e' in mathematics? Stand up the boy who put the 'e' in mathematics. I have been at Burgrove for seven years and in all my seven years at Burgrove I have never had such a thing happen. Never. The long and short of it is that Gilbert was in Faggott's room and Faggott was there and we all sang. I had a whisky and Faggott sang. I like Faggott and I had a whisky because he is going away. Mind you, there was a time when things were different. Not the same. But now they are the same all right and I like Faggott. Then he sang again and I had another whisky because I like him. While he was singing I told him so. 'I bear no grudge,' I said, and he was pleased. Then we all had whiskies and I sang. We all sang. They all sang. He was about to have sung. *Cano – canare.* CANARY! See the point, Mason? *cano* – canary – cantuar. The Archbishop of Canterbury sang!

I fell in a puddle and tore my trousers. The fact of the matter is that Faggott was drunk. Faggott was drunk when he went to see the Headmaster and I ran after him to stop him. Good old Faggott. They tried to prevent me but I ran after him and fell into a puddle in the dark and tore my trousers. So I did not catch him until he reached the Headmaster's door. I seized his coat-tails as he was going in and he lost his balance and fell, but he did not tear his trousers. I am certain of that. He simply fell backwards on the floor and lay there while I spoke to the Headmaster. I went straight up to the Headmaster and took him by the lapels. 'I bear no grudge, Headmaster,' I said. He did not seem to understand, so I showed him the state of my trousers and asked him what in the world he thought Matron would have to say about them. Then Faggott pushed me aside. I was upset and began to sing 'Asleep in the Deep'. Anybody would. But after a while the Headmaster came up and told me to go back to my room at once and get to bed. He said that unless such a thing ever happened again he would say no more about it. He will regret that. I pointed out that I was Senior Mathematics master at Burgrove Preparatory School, which was true. But his attitude was contumacious. I told him his attitude was contumelious. Then I said good night, as I had done all I could for Faggott for the time being. When I had got out of the room I remembered something and went back.

'It's about my trousers, Headmaster,' I said. That is what I resent so bitterly. I have done my best and the Headmaster's attitude is contumelious, as I told him. Afterwards...

Summer Term 1939
Prelude to Disaster

Nothing, I suppose, can now stop the story getting about. I blame the Headmaster for this. Had he listened quietly to my explanation, as I think I had a right to expect, instead of wilfully misinterpreting the situation in which he chanced to find me, the whole ridiculous affair would have been cleared up, my coat would have been on and the fishing-rod back in its place long before Wilson and Tremayne peeped into the boot-room. As it is, goodness knows what wild rumours the boys will spread about the incident. Already some young ass has chalked 'LOBSTER POTS. KEEP OFF' on the top of the boot-lockers; the next thing I suppose will be ground-bait on the floor of my form-room and similar follies. Well, I shall know how to deal with that kind of humour.

Looking back I cannot see that I acted unwisely at any point, given the unusual circumstances in which I found myself. If the Headmaster cannot understand why I should want my umbrella at eleven o'clock at night, it shows a want of sensibility on his part, not any lack of sense on mine. The fact is that I did *not* want my umbrella, in one way, for it was a fine starlight night and I had nowhere to go – unless it had occurred to me to go for a walk at that improbable hour of night – which I should never have done had it been raining, naturally. I simply wanted to know where my umbrella was.

I had expected it to be down at the Cottage, actually, but noticing quite by chance that it was not in its usual corner in the hall I had a hunt in my bedroom and still failed to find it. I became rather worried and as it was a fine night decided to set my mind at rest by strolling up to the school and having a look in the Common Room cupboard – not the cupboard *in* the Common Room, where we keep our gowns, but the tall one just outside where cricket bats and so on are kept in the winter and footballs in the summer. What the Headmaster cannot seem to see is that it was only *because* it was a fine night that I was looking for it at all. It would have been madness to walk up to School through a downpour simply to see whether my umbrella was there or not.

At any rate I went straight to the cupboard, not troubling to switch on the lights for I had my torch with me, and had just ascertained that my umbrella was *not* there when I stepped back on to a cricket ball, and, in saving myself from a tumble, had the ill-fortune to smash my torch against the wall. So I had to grope my way out of the cupboard in the dark and in doing so dislodged Gilbert's fishing-rod which fell with a clatter to the floor. Rather carelessly, in my opinion, though I am no fisher-man, he keeps it set up ready for an occasional afternoon with the grayling, instead of taking it to pieces when he has finished with it. Luckily I found the rod after a little trouble, by sweeping about with my hands, and stood it up again in its corner. Then I turned to go out, but to my astonishment as I moved the rod fell down again. When the same thing happened a third time I decided to leave the rod where it was until I had put the lights on and could see what the trouble was. I had not yet realized of course what had happened. But the moment I took a step into the corridor I felt something pluck sharply at my clothing at the back and a kind of grating scream came out of the depths of the cupboard. I am not easily rattled – I should hardly be a schoolmaster if I were – but I confess that for a moment my blood ran cold. Then I pulled myself together, put my hand behind my back and grasped the gut that was holding me fast to Gilbert's rod and reel.

By ill-chance the hook had caught me firmly between the shoulder blades, out of reach, and though I might have broken the gut I did not care, except as a last resort, deliberately to damage a colleague's property. I was now in something of a dilemma. Had it been merely a question of getting to the light-switch in the corridor the problem would have been relatively simple; but it was not, for all downstairs lights in the school buildings are controlled by a master-switch behind the boot-room door, and this the Headmaster himself switches off every evening at half-past ten. It was out of the question to attempt to make my way to the boot-room with the reel screaming behind me at every step. I should have woken every boy in the house. I therefore decided, as I think rightly, to take the rod with me to the boot-room (carrying it of course in my hand). To avoid further noise I re-entered the cupboard backwards on my hands and knees, or rather on my knees and right hand, for with my left I kept contact with the line. In this way I had no difficulty in finding the tip of the rod. Then working my fingers down until I grasped the butt I rose to my feet and left the cupboard for the last time.

It was no easy journey to the boot-room. If I raised the point of the rod too high the result was a sharp tug at my shoulders and a warning scream from the reel, while to lower it too much was to run the risk of entanglement in the slack. It was, I suppose, fear of this latter disaster that made me raise the point too sharply after manoeuvring it carefully through the boot-room door. Unknown to me, the line at the very tip of the rod looped itself round the hasp of the fan-light over the door, and inevitably at my next step forward the coat rose on my back, the rod quivered in my hands and a yard of line was stripped with great violence from the reel.

There was now only one thing to be done. I leaned the rod against the door-jamb, removed my coat and lowered it with great care to the floor, at the same time keeping one hand on the rod in case it should be pulled over by the movement of the coat. I was now of course free and very soon had the master-switch down and the boot-room light working. Then I picked up the rod and, stepping on to the boot-lockers, lifted the line clear of the fan-light hasp.

That the Head should appear at this moment was only in keeping, I suppose, with the miserable ill-fortune I had met with all through.

'Ah, Wentworth,' he said. 'I thought I heard a noise.' Then his eyebrows went up.

'Do you often come here to fish?' he asked.

'I was worried about my umbrella, sir,' I began, realizing at once that until he knew what had happened my behaviour must seem very odd, 'and as it is a fine night – ' but he cut my explanation short.

'I see,' he said. 'And you thought a little fishing would take your mind off your worries? You have foul-hooked your coat, I notice.'

'This rod was in the Common Room cupboard, Headmaster,' I explained, stepping down off the lockers, 'and as you can see, the hook caught my coat while I was looking for my umbrella. It is Gilbert's rod,' I added.

The Headmaster still looked dubious. 'It's a long cast from the cupboard to the boot-room, Wentworth,' he objected.

'My coat was in the cupboard, sir,' I said with some impatience. 'If you would allow me to explain the whole thing – '

'No, no,' he said. 'No. I don't wish to pry into my masters' affairs. I have no objection whatever to your fishing in the cupboard, provided the boys are not disturbed. But I do think it ought to stop there. I *cannot* understand how you come to be in your shirt-sleeves in the boot-room, considering – What do *you* want?'

He had turned sharply, and to my dismay I caught a glimpse over his shoulder of Wilson and Tremayne in their dressing-gowns.

'I – we're sorry, sir,' said Tremayne, looking at my fishing-rod with his eyes popping out of his head. 'I didn't know – we thought we heard a queer noise – '

'Get off to bed, both of you, at once,' ordered the Headmaster, and when they had run off, he turned back to me and made the most inexplicable remark.

'You and your umbrella, Wentworth,' he said. 'You'll be the death of me yet.'

What is particularly puzzling is that this is the first occasion, so far as I know, on which I have even mentioned my umbrella to the Headmaster.

WEDNESDAY, 17 MAY

'A train,' I read out to my IIIA boys, 'leaves Edinburgh for Glasgow at half-past three, arriving at its destination – Well, what *is* it, Etheridge?'

I understood him to say that the half-past three from Edinburgh now left at quarter to four, or some such rubbish.

'Are you trying to be funny?' I demanded sternly.

I think he was genuinely surprised by my attitude, for he flushed up to the roots of his hair and answered quite seriously, 'Good lord, no, sir. It's the summer time-tables, sir. They've put the three-thirty Glasgow train back fifteen minutes so as to connect with the one-fifty-two – '

'Etheridge lives in Edinburgh, sir,' explained Mason in his interfering way.

'He's nuts on *Bradshaw*, too,' added Atkins. 'I'll bet he's right, sir.'

I thanked them all for their assistance, and pointed out that for the purposes of the problem I was about to ask them to be good enough to undertake, it was really immaterial whether Etheridge lived in Edinburgh or Clacton-on-Sea. 'Nor,' I added to clinch the matter, 'do I care a brass farthing if *Bradshaw* says the half-past three train starts at breakfast-time. *I'm* not "nuts on *Bradshaw*", Atkins.'

'I only thought we might as well have it right, sir,' said Etheridge.

'Can't you see, you little nanny-goat,' I cried in exasperation, 'that we are not concerned with what actually happens *now*! I am giving out a sum, not arranging a Sunday outing on the Clyde.'

'Oh, Sunday?' Etheridge said. 'She doesn't run on Sundays.'

'I see,' I said ironically; 'she doesn't run on Sundays. Well, if everybody has made a note of that important fact, perhaps we can get on with our work. Doesn't run on Sundays, indeed! We shall have Mason asking for a non-smoker, next.'

When the laughter raised by this sally had died down I gave them the remaining details of the problem, namely that the three-thirty arrives in Glasgow at five o'clock whereas a train leaving Glasgow at the same time reaches Edinburgh in exactly two hours. The distance between the two places is given as sixty miles (Etheridge opened his silly mouth at this, but I quietened him with a frown), and the problem is of course to discover at what distance from Edinburgh the two trains meet.

I had hardly finished speaking before Williamson, rather an obtuse boy, began to protest that they couldn't do that without knowing the speed of the trains.

'*Think*, boy,' I implored him. 'How far apart are the two stations? Sixty miles? Right, and how long does the train from Glasgow to Edinburgh take?

86

Two hours, doesn't it? Very well, then. Now, can you tell me the speed in miles per hour?'

'No, sir.'

'No, Williamson?'

'No, sir. At least – no, sir, not unless I know how often the train stops.'

'There are no stops whatever, Williamson,' I told him wearily. 'You can take it that the train is an express.'

'Sixty miles in two hours!' cried Mason. 'Golly, what a flier!'

'Get on, Mason,' I said sharply. 'All right now, Williamson?'

'I think so, thank you, sir. Except what about the other train, the one going from Edinburgh, the three-thirty, sir?'

'They're both three-thirties, fool,' said somebody, but though I whipped round like a flash I wasn't quick enough to catch him.

'What about it?' I asked, returning to Williamson.

'I mean, does it stop?'

'It stops at Airdrie,' put in Etheridge before I could speak. 'If you mean the three-forty-five, that is.'

'In here at two-thirty sharp, Etheridge,' I ordered, losing patience. 'And you too, Mason, if you can't stop that idiotic grinning. We are wasting far too much time. Both trains – you'd better listen to this all of you, because I'm not going to answer any more questions – both trains are expresses and run at a constant speed from start to finish.'

'In that case, sir,' objected Atkins, 'I don't see why one of them gets there first.'

'Tell him, somebody.'

'Because it's got farther to go,' suggested Williamson.

'Oh, jolly good, Batty!' one of them shouted, and not being able to think of a better comment myself I let it pass.

Shortly after this I left the form-room for a moment, ostensibly to fetch a book from the Common Room, but in reality to stop the boys asking questions and force them to work the difficulties out for themselves. In the corridor I met the Headmaster.

'Hullo, Wentworth,' he greeted me, taking my elbow. 'I've been wanting a word with you. You never told me the real history of that fishing trip of yours the other night. I'm dying to know.'

'As I think I told you in the boot-room at the time, Headmaster,' I began stiffly, 'I was merely looking for my umbrella – '

'*Because* it was a fine night.'

'Exactly. And as – '

'Did you find it?'

'No,' I said. 'Unfortunately not. It was extremely dark in the cupboard as you can imagine – '

'And you took Gilbert's rod by mistake? I see.'

'There was no mistake about it, Headmaster,' I

said warmly. 'I may be all kinds of a fool, but I can still distinguish between my umbrella and a nine-foot fishing-rod, I am thankful to say.'

'Then you took the rod to the boot-room on purpose?'

'The point is,' I explained, 'that I could not leave the cupboard without it. So, rather than spend the whole night in the cupboard, I took it with me.'

'Remember, a term or two ago, how you took a maidenhair fern out of my study, Wentworth? I thought at the time it was some sort of un-controllable impulse that came over you, and I suppose this – this sudden desire to fish comes in the same category, eh?'

But for a twinkle in the Headmaster's eye I should have been seriously annoyed at this reference to a silly misunderstanding that once occurred over a pot-plant of his. Not that the plant was of any particular value to me or anyone else, as it happened.

'If you would let me show you exactly what happened, Headmaster?' I suggested.

He turned away and stood with his back to me for a while, looking out over the playing fields.

'You mean,' he said at last, turning round with an expression I could not quite fathom, 'you mean – go in the cupboard again?'

I nodded, and he at once agreed to come and watch my demonstration after lunch.

'Half-past two, Wentworth,' he said, adding

rather inconsequently, 'I'll send the School out for a walk.'

Thinking it over, I am not sure that I have been wise; I doubt whether any good will come of it. For one thing, of course, I have had to let Mason and Etheridge off detention.

WENTWORTH RE-ENTERS THE CUPBOARD

[*I am indebted to Mr Charles Gilbert for the following account of what took place that afternoon. Mr Wentworth himself is silent on the point.*]

Anybody who has known Wentworth for more than a couple of minutes is aware that however much of a clown he makes of himself, whatever fantastic predicament he gets into, he will not leave the thing alone. He will not rest until he has proved to his own satisfaction, and attempted to convince everybody else, that the whole affair was perfectly natural really. If he was found hanging by his braces from the dome of St Paul's (and nobody here would be the least surprised if he were) he would put it down to negligence on the part of the Dean, coupled with a certain amount of sheer bad luck on his own part. 'In attempting,' he would say, 'to make my way out of the Whispering Gallery I had the misfortune to catch my foot....'

Undoubtedly it was this feeling that led Wentworth to give a demonstration to the Headmaster of the way in which he got snared in my fishing-line, and to show how inevitably this mischance compelled him to climb on to the lockers in the boot-room, with my rod in his hand, and his coat, firmly hooked, gasping out its life on the floor.

Rawlinson and I knew nothing about this demonstration, as a matter of fact, until just before it was due to begin. We happened to be talking to Wentworth, who was hanging about outside the cupboard by the Common Room door, when the Headmaster came along.

'Ah, Wentworth,' he said. 'I see you've got quite a gathering for it.'

'Gilbert and Rawlinson are just off for a walk, sir,' Wentworth explained.

'No hurry,' I said, 'if we can be of any use.'

'Well, Gilbert,' old Saunders said, 'you ought to be present, as it was your rod,' and he explained, not without a certain difficulty in controlling his voice, what Wentworth was going to do.

So we saw the whole thing.

Wentworth began with a long rigmarole, which I cannot attempt to follow in detail, about his umbrella. The upshot of it seemed to be that as he didn't want it the sensible thing to do was to come up in the dark and look for it in the games cupboard. Asked by Rawlinson whether he kept his umbrella in the games cupboard, he said, 'Of course not,' which settled that point. Then he went into the cupboard, still talking.

'You can imagine, Headmaster, that when I lost the use of my torch it was pitch dark in here. It is pretty dark in here now, even by day, as you can see.'

We all crowded into the cupboard after him, to see just how dark it was, and Rawlinson, with a stroke of genius, shut the door 'in order to reproduce as closely as possible the actual conditions'. It was now very dark indeed, and we were jammed so tightly together that I could distinctly feel old Saunders shaking all over with suppressed laughter. I was, as a matter of fact, shaking myself.

'What did you do then, Wentworth?'

'My first thought naturally, Headmaster, was to get some light, and I therefore made my way – I beg your pardon, sir.'

'It's all right,' said Rawlinson, 'that was *my* foot.'

'If we could have a little light – Ah! What's this?' There was a slight clatter and almost simultaneously I was butted violently by Wentworth, who appeared to be sweeping the floor with his hands.

'Let go my leg,' cried the Headmaster suddenly, and immediately burst into uncontrollable laughter. Only Wentworth was still able to speak and he, in rather a querulous voice, kept asking why somebody didn't open the door.

Somebody did, from the outside, and we heard the indignant voice of Miss Coombes (our music lady) demanding 'What are you boys doing in there? Come out at once!'

I doubt if a more sheepish lot ever trailed out of a cupboard than the Headmaster and staff of

Burgrove Preparatory School.

'Why, Mr Saunders!' she cried. 'I – I'm sorry to – to have interrupted you, but I thought perhaps –'

It was an awkward little scene. Only Wentworth, who has been through too much, I suppose, to be concerned about a straightforward situation like this, looked altogether at ease.

'I've got it, you see, Miss Coombes,' he said, flourishing his umbrella. 'I had an idea it might be in there, all along.'

When Miss Coombes had left us, very red in the face, the Headmaster rounded on Wentworth.

'So that's what you had round my ankle, you old rascal. You would have had me over, if there had been any room to fall down in.'

Wentworth pointed out gravely that there had of course been more room on the night he had first looked for his umbrella. 'I was by myself, you see,' he explained, and we agreed that this was just as well.

The rest of the demonstration went off almost without a hitch. We got him hooked up, as directed, and off he went with a March Brown firmly anchored in his coat at the back and my rod clasped in his right hand – exactly as on the night, except that he was not on that occasion carrying his umbrella as well.

He showed us how, on entering the boot-room in search of the light-switch, he had raised the point of the rod too high and so, 'as ill-luck would have it', got the top of the line looped round the hasp on the fan-light. He had first become aware of this, 'you will understand, Headmaster,' when he felt a jerk and heard more line screaming off the reel; and he demonstrated the jerk and the scream most convincingly. But he failed to notice, and we felt it unnecessary to point out, that on this occasion the reel had overrun, so that a loop of slack line was left hanging between the reel and the first eye on the rod.

I need hardly say that Wentworth put his foot through this loop. It is a fairly easy thing to do, but nobody could have done it more easily than he did.

'Hullo!' he said. 'I'm caught.'

'Did this happen when – on the night?' we asked.

'No. Oh, no,' he said, smiling. 'This is an unrehearsed effect.'

He was standing on one leg now, trying to scrape the line off his right calf with the point of his umbrella. When he began to lose his balance I had a moment's uneasiness, for I feared he might put his right foot down too abruptly, trying to save himself, and thereby snap the point of the rod. But I need not have worried. With the umbrella between his legs he never had a chance, and after spinning right round twice like a top he had to confess himself beaten and went down with all hands into the boot-basket.

'Are you hurt, old chap?' I asked, as soon as I

could speak.

'No, no,' he said, struggling to get up. 'I am all right, thank you. But I am worried about my umbrella.'

'You said that the first time,' cried the Headmaster, and rushed off hooting, I regret to say, like a madman.

We could hear him, far off down the corridor, beating his knees with his hands and repeating at intervals with a kind of incredulous awe, 'He's worried about his umbrella! Oh, my aunt, he's *still* worried about his umbrella!'

FRIDAY, 23 JUNE – EVE OF FOUNDATION DAY

I felt tired and depressed when I woke up today. The depression lasted all morning and I found it difficult to concentrate on my work, with the result that in working out a sum concerning the price of eggs my mind wandered to the wall-papering problems which we did last week. This led me to attempt to find the perimeter of the eggs in feet and inches, which of course, not knowing the measurement of the eggs, I could not do. I rubbed it all out and began again but was still muddled and got an answer giving the number of eggs (which of course we knew already) instead of their price. Very unwillingly, for I dislike anything that savours of subterfuge, I explained to the boys that I had done this in order to test them and called Mason up to point out where I had gone wrong. He said that he couldn't see anything wrong with it except that it was a mistake to try to paper a room with eggs – at which we all laughed. He asked for a mark, which I allowed, perhaps unjustifiably, but I was in no mood for argument, and I offered to double it if he could work out the sum correctly himself. He said, 'Let x be an egg.'

I told Etheridge to stop tittering and nodded to Mason.

'Well, sir, then twelve eggs equal $12x$.

'Well?'

'Then 94 eggs equal $12x$ multiplied by 94 over 12, that's to say, sir – er – 94 eggs equal – um – $94x$.'

'I see,' I said. 'So 94 eggs equal $94x$. Go on.'

'So, you see, sir, as 94 eggs cost ten shillings therefore $94x$ equals ten. Then if the price goes up a halfpenny a dozen, the cost of a gross – at least, wait a minute, sir, if 94 eggs equal $94x$ then surely x equals one?'

'One what?'

'One egg, sir.'

I threw up my hands. 'What on earth is the good of that, Mason?' I asked.

The boy looked genuinely surprised. 'That's the value of x, sir. I thought that's what you wanted.'

'Do you mean to say that that is your answer?'

He said it was, and when I told him to sit down, calmly asked for another mark. It is this kind of attitude that makes a schoolmaster's task so unnecessarily difficult and wearing. Boys like Mason make no attempt to get to the root of a problem, they simply let x equal anything that occurs to them, whether it has any bearing on the sum or not, and imagine that by multiplying and dividing it they will arrive at some sort of answer and perhaps get a mark for their trouble. Naturally it is particularly annoying to find them using x in a sum of this kind which does not call for the introduction of an unknown quantity. I worked the problem out again myself, getting it right this time – only to find Hillman drawing horses on his blotting-paper (a silly trick) and Hopgood II asleep. There is something wrong with Hopgood II, I think, but whenever I speak to Matron about his drowsiness she merely says that none of the other masters have complained of his going to sleep in their forms. As if that had anything to do with it.

After dinner this evening I went to see the Head on some small point about Common Entrance papers, forgetting that tomorrow is Foundation Day here and that the Bishop of Saintsbury, who has kindly consented to preach at the morning service, would naturally be staying the night. However, the Headmaster made me welcome, cutting short my attempted explanations with a genial 'No shop now, Wentworth!' and invited me to take coffee with them. I accepted and we had a pleasant chat.

The Bishop seems to be a man with wide interests, not at all 'churchy' or wrapped up in narrow diocesan affairs. He was talking about the Bren gun when I came in and good-naturedly included me in the conversation by asking whether I could tell him the average life of the barrel. I said I had no idea, and asked him in my turn whether he by any chance knew a Canon Slinford, who had, I believed, or used to have, associations with Saintsbury. He said he did not, but he knew, of course, Lady Slinford, the niece of the Earl of Belsize, who had recently married one of the Worcestershire Frumps – or some such name. I replied with a smile that so far as I knew the Canon was not connected with any noble family, whereupon he turned to the Headmaster and began to talk to him about Swedish pom-poms – all Greek to me. Apparently the Bishop had been dining recently with a member of the Cabinet who told him in confidence that their manufacture was going ahead by leaps and bounds. Then the conversation turned to tanks. Mr Saunders ventured to observe that he supposed the day of the horse in warfare was over, but with this the Bishop could not altogether agree.

Hearing the horse mentioned and not wishing to be left out of the conversation, I quoted the first apposite line from the Bible which came into my head, 'The glory of his nostrils is terrible.'

'Whom do you mean, sir?' asked the Bishop, wheeling round.

I explained that I meant the horse and added 'Ha Ha among the trumpets' to make the reference clear. Our visitor replied with a grunt and seeing that he was becoming tired, not unnaturally, of this rather military talk, I put a question to him about his diocese, which I had always understood to be largely agricultural and therefore at the moment going, perhaps, through a rather difficult time. But he misunderstood my meaning, replying that the chief trouble was a serious shortage of ambulance drivers and quoting figures which seemed to relate, so far as I could follow them, to the Auxiliary Fire Brigade. This talking at cross-purposes confused me and I said good night and took my leave without remembering to ask, as I had intended, about the Lessons for tomorrow. Presumably the Headmaster will read the second, leaving 'Let us now praise famous men' to me, in the ordinary way, but it is just possible he may wish to spare his voice, in view of his Speech, and in that case Rawlinson should, I suppose, be warned. I returned to the study to make sure, but finding the Bishop on the floor expounding some point in connexion with high-angle fire, crept out again without disturbing him.

It is all rather puzzling. But no doubt everything will go off splendidly tomorrow.

SATURDAY, 24 JUNE – FOUNDATION DAY

And what a day it has been! No school, of course, but a great deal to arrange and the prizes to see to, and so on. It wouldn't do to have any hitch at the last moment with all the parents in their places and our whole organization *sub judice* so to speak, or whatever the expression is. There *was* a bit of a difficulty, as a matter of fact, because the wrong *Decline and Fall* had been sent – nothing to do with the Roman Empire as far as I could see on a hasty inspection, and in places hardly suitable for young boys. When I pointed this out to the Headmaster immediately after breakfast, he laughed and said it was lucky they hadn't sent the right one or we should never have got it all into the gym (where we have the prize-giving nowadays).

'But what are we to do, Headmaster?' I asked. 'Baylis will be terribly disappointed if there is no prize for him.'

He said he was very busy and had every confidence in my ability to do what seemed best – all very well, but I cannot be expected to conjure books out of thin air, especially on a day like this when I have enough to do in all conscience and the whole place is swarming with parents determined to get hold of one and talk about their boys. However, I managed to find Thring, whose parents are in India, and arranged that after receiving his copy of *Ivanhoe* he should hand it at once to one of the senior boys who would unobtrusively return it to the table. It could then be presented again to Baylis when his turn came and nobody need be any the wiser. Of course I promised that Thring should have another copy as soon as it could be obtained. He asked if he might have *Forty Years Under the Sea*, or some such book, instead. I had never heard of it and doubted whether it would have the same appeal for a boy as *Ivanhoe*, so I gave a non-committal reply. I don't see that I could have made any better arrangement on the spur of the moment.

Just before Chapel I met the Bishop taking a stroll down the Avenue and put some casual question to him about Consistory Courts, merely as a means of opening a conversation. To my astonishment be burst into a torrent of what I should have described, in one not of his cloth, as angry abuse, asking me what the dickens I thought I was playing at, whether I imagined he was the Archbishop of Canterbury in disguise or what, and a lot more incomprehensible questions. 'But surely,' I said, 'you are the Bishop of Saintsbury?'

It turns out that he is not a bishop at all, but a retired Colonel who has taken Orders late in life 'for want,' as he chose to put it, 'of something better to do.' How Gilbert, who definitely told me that the Bishop of Saintsbury was coming down to preach on Foundation Day, came to make the mistake I do not pretend to know. Naturally when I called on the Headmaster last night and discovered a gentleman in clerical dress in his study I took it for granted that his guest was the Bishop. It is true I might have paused to wonder why he was not in apron and gaiters, but the fact of the matter is I simply failed to notice. After all it is no business of mine what bishops wear. I have enough to worry about already without that.

'Why then, Colonel,' I said, after begging his pardon for mistaking him for a Bishop (an error which seemed to fill him with quite unreasonable resentment), 'I wonder if, in your professional capacity, you ever came across a Major Faggott, who was on the staff here a short while ago?'

'Faggott?' he said, 'Faggott? No, never heard of him. Not one of ours, anyway.'

'Whose?' I asked.

'Ours.'

'Oh!' I said, rather at a loss. 'Not one of ours either, really.'

This for some reason made the Colonel think I was an old Army man myself, and after a few minutes' rather fruitless conversation we parted. His sermon, which took the form of an appeal to us all to join the Territorial Army, was rather wasted on the boys, who have all made up their minds to become Air Cadets as soon as they are old enough. Still, he is of course an Old Boy, and we were all glad he was able to come.

I thought the Headmaster's speech went better than ever this year. The parents were obviously pleased at his reference to the health of the school, which, apart from influenza and the mumps epidemic last term, has been uniformly excellent, and they clapped very heartily at the announcement of special Rhythmic Exercise classes in the near future for boys who wish to take them. In games, the Headmaster said, the school had not perhaps been quite so successful as in some previous years, but the general level of performance throughout the school had never, he thought, been higher, and that, after all, was of more importance than the possession of a few boys of outstanding ability in the First Elevens. Turning to work he explained that with an unusually young Sixth Form the Honours List was necessarily a short one; they would all be getting their scholarships next year. But he had much pleasure in congratulating Thomas on his successful entry into the Royal Naval College, Dartmouth. In conclusion he very kindly mentioned the unfailing assistance and loyal support he had received from every member of the Staff.

Afterwards Lady Portcullis gave away the prizes. Hillman, I was glad to see, got the Tidiest Dormitory Prize in his capacity as Aedile of the Junior Green. Aediles, of course, have not the authority of full Praetors (of which there are six), but are put in charge of the smaller dormitories such as the Junior Green, Admiral Benbow and Upper Far – which used to be called Eastman's until the tragedy. There was, after all, a muddle about Baylis's prize, because Thring, apparently misunderstanding my instructions, handed his *Ivanhoe* to Baylis, who was sitting near him, directly he returned to his seat. Then Baylis, when his name was called out by the Headmaster, took the book up with him and gave it back to Lady Portcullis. This naturally confused Lady Portcullis who had just been handed *The Lays of Ancient Rome* (intended as a matter of fact for Thomas) by the Headmaster and, no doubt in order to cover up a moment's hesitation, she asked the boy, very kindly, what his name was. He said it was Thomas, meaning his Christian name, of course (he is quite a little chap really – only nine), and she thereupon gave him *The Lays*, at the same time congratulating him in a clear voice on passing into the Navy. Baylis got very red, but wisely said nothing. This left *Ivanhoe* for Thomas – I mean Thomas, R., of the Upper IV – as his prize for passing the Dartmouth Entrance. He accepted it without comment, though I happen to know that he received a copy of the same novel last term for his work in Set I. Still, there was nothing else to be done.

On the whole a most successful Speech and Prize-giving.

The Old Boys beat the School by three wickets this afternoon. An excellent game, though I confess my attention was rather distracted at times. Several parents came up to discuss their sons' progress, and in particular I had a long talk with Mrs Hillman. She is petite with blue eyes and is rather charming though a little unorthodox. We talked about ballet for a while, of which I know nothing, and then she suddenly turned to me and remarked, 'What a funny old stick your headmaster is!' I was naturally taken aback, especially as other parents and their boys were standing quite close to us, and I hurriedly observed that I hoped she would be at the concert in the evening. But she refused to take the hint.

'Come now, Mr Wentworth,' she said, laying her small hand on my arm, 'you can't deny it. Look at him talking to that woman in the wig over there.'

'Really, Mrs Hillman!' I said in a low voice. 'We are not alone.'

'That isn't my fault, is it, Mr Wentworth?' she replied.

I was absolutely dumbfounded, and before I could collect my wits she went on in the most confiding way, 'Is he or is he not a pompous old thing?'

'Well – ' I began, and we both laughed.

We soon became firm friends and she talked in a most interesting way about several of the parents, many of whom she seemed to know personally. I pointed out Clarke's mother, a very striking figure in red, and she remarked, 'It costs that woman eight hundred a year to look like that.'

'No one would say that of you, Mrs Hillman,' I said gallantly.

'Meaning that I'm obviously cheaply turned-out?' she replied mischievously.

I simply gave her a look and she lowered her eyes.

'Here comes that spiteful old cat with the wig,' she said presently. 'Now watch. Hullo, Peggy. You know Mr Wentworth, don't you? Mr Wentworth – Lady Cleethorpes.'

'How do you do,' I said.

'We were just talking about you,' said Mrs Hillman. 'Mr Wentworth was saying you looked a spiteful old cat.'

'I assure you, Lady Cleethorpes!' I cried, reddening to the roots of my hair. 'Mrs Hillman is utterly – '

'Did she tell you I wear a wig?'

'I – that is,' I began, completely at a loss for words, 'I should never have guessed – '

'Well, I don't,' said Lady Cleethorpes, and both women went off into peals of laughter.

I felt extremely uncomfortable. People were looking at us – and no wonder. The cricket field, when a serious game is in progress, is not the place for loud laughter. Besides, the whole position was most embarrassing. There seemed to be no knowing what these extraordinary ladies would say next. I determined to bring the conversation back to a sensible level at once.

'How is your husband, Mrs Hillman?' I asked, giving her a reproachful look.

She became serious at once. 'I have no husband – now, Mr Wentworth,' she said.

I murmured a few conventional words of sympathy, cursing myself silently for a clumsy fool, but she cut me short.

'I divorced him,' she said briskly. 'He was no loss.'

'So go in and win, Mr Wentworth,' added Lady Cleethorpes with another of her penetrating laughs.

I may be old-fashioned but I confess I have no use whatever for this kind of talk. Divorce is not a subject for jesting. No doubt, in the world in which some people live, the so-called *haut monde*, it is considered clever and amusing to make light of serious and intimate subjects of this kind, but here at Burgrove we prefer to take a different attitude. Moreover I do not care to be made the object of remarks in, to say the least, doubtful taste, particularly when these involve the good name of a lady who happens to be present.

I made my excuses rather coldly and turned away, not knowing that one of my sock-suspenders had unluckily come unfastened and was trailing on the ground. I might not have noticed had not Mrs Hillman unwittingly set her foot on the metal clasp or fastener so that I was brought up short after a single stride and all but overbalanced.

Mrs Hillman very kindly moved her foot in a quite natural way when she noticed my predicament, as if unaware that anything unusual had happened, but Lady Cleethorpes, who seems to be utterly lacking in tact, broke out into another loud laugh and cried, 'You'll have to marry her now.' This was too much for my temper and I fear I might have spoken very sharply to Lady Cleethorpes had not the Headmaster come up at that moment and joined the group.

'Ah!' he said, rubbing his hands together in a way which I am bound to say I sometimes find rather irritating, 'I hope Mr Wentworth has been entertaining you two ladies.'

'He certainly has,' said Lady Cleethorpes.

I left them as soon as I could and wandered off to the far side of the field, where I did my best to forget my annoyance by concentrating on the game. The Old Boys had got to within twenty-five of our total for the loss of four wickets, mainly through Felpman (a mainstay of the Eleven in the old days, though a poor mathematician. Percentages always used to beat him, I remember), and things looked bad for Burgrove. Then Clarke stopped a hot one at extra cover and I joined in the general shouts of 'Play up, School!' Nothing came of it, however.

'Oh, Mr Wentworth,' said a well-known voice, and I turned to find Mrs Hillman at my side. 'I am so sorry,' she said, 'if Peggy annoyed you.'

'It was nothing,' I said stiffly. 'Lady Cleethorpes has perhaps a rather – unusual sense of humour.'

'You're not angry with me, are you?'

I looked down at her kindly, and found to my intense mortification that I was still holding the loose suspender in my right hand. Mrs Hillman followed the direction of my eyes and then, with a discretion that I admired, turned her head away. I stuffed the offending article into my pocket.

'Tell me, Mrs Hillman,' I said, to cover our mutual embarrassment; 'your friend – Lady Cleethorpes – she has no boy here surely? There is no Cleethorpes on the School List. A nephew perhaps?'

'Oh, didn't you know?' she replied, opening her eyes wide in astonishment. 'That's her son over there – that tall good-looking boy in spectacles. She used to be a Mrs Mason before her second marriage, you know.'

'*Mason?*' I cried.

'Yes. Johnny Mason. You must know him.'

'Ah!' I said. 'Yes. Yes, yes. Mason! I see.'

[*Two weeks later occurred the unfortunate affair of Hopgood II and the algebra book which might have had serious consequences for Wentworth's career but for the general amnesty which a world war brings in its train. Early in 1940 he joined the army. A few scattered extracts from the diary of Second-Lieut. Wentworth, R.A. will be found in the next section of this book.*]

An Assistant Master at War

I fell over that coil of rubber tubing again this morning on my way back after inspecting the cookhouse and went straight off and reported it to the Adjutant. The thing is simply a deathtrap where it is at present. He said, 'Get it moved, then. You're Orderly Officer at this R.H.Q., aren't you?'

I pointed out that I should hardly care to move a piece of equipment without his authority, but that if he gave that authority I would have it moved at once.

'All right,' he said, 'go ahead and move it. And for goodness' sake, Wentworth, don't come and bother me about every trivial thing that crops up. I'm busy.'

I thought this unfair. It is very difficult for a new officer to know just what he may or may not do without reference to higher authority. I determined to get things clear in my mind once for all.

'May I take it then, sir,' I asked, 'that in future I have authority to move such things as coils of tubing and so on without applying to you?'

'Yes, yes, yes,' he said.

'What about benches and tables?'

'Do you want to move benches and tables, Wentworth?'

'No,' I said. 'But the occasion might arise.'

'Well, when it does arise, for the Lord's sake move them!'

'On my own initiative?'

'On your own flat feet for all I care,' said the Adjutant, throwing down his pen.

'Very good, sir,' I said, keeping my temper, and saluted, not noticing a tray of papers which had very foolishly been placed on top of a filing-cabinet at my right elbow. It took me some little time to collect all the papers and replace them. I am not a young man and quite unused to scrambling about under desks on all-fours. We left that kind of thing to the boys at Burgrove, I am thankful to say. But war is no respecter of persons; I quite realize that.

It was this little contretemps, I think, that made me forget, until I was outside the door, that one point still remained to be settled, and I had therefore to re-enter in order to ask where I was to put the rubber tubing.

To my mind the Adjutant's reply was absolutely inexcusable. No doubt he is a busy man; we are all busy these days. But if I am prepared to take the trouble to ask him a civil question in order to ensure that I carry out my duties correctly, the least he can do is to give a civil answer. After all, we are all in this war to help one another, are we not? Without co-operation, as I tried to tell him, the whole system falls to the ground. Besides, he was the first to complain over that business of the cinders last week. I remember his very words: 'Next time you are thinking of having a lot of smouldering ashes emptied in the ammunition store, just advise me about it beforehand, will you, Wentworth?' Very well. It was simply because of a natural anxiety to avoid any similar misunderstanding over the rubber tubing that I put my question. Surely I had a right to expect a reasonable reply?

I have half a mind to make a complaint.

THURSDAY, 27 MARCH 1941

Old Poole is back at the school, so I hear in a note from Rawlinson. Dear old chap. He left us in 1937 and has come back, I suppose, to take Collingridge's place now the latter has gone into the Navy. I don't know, I'm sure. Collingridge was our English master and Poole taught only French – and not very much of that, I'm afraid – so I don't see how it is going to work out. Probably they will share out Collingridge's work between Rawlinson and that new man Bishop. But then who is going to take IVB? It is all very muddling.

I have been driven almost to distraction by that confounded rubber tubing. I had it put in the miniature rifle range, which has been used as a dump for all kinds of unwanted bales and boxes ever since the war began; but apparently there is a plan to use the range for shooting, and somebody threw the tubing out again into the middle of the drill hall. There the Adjutant found it and made quite a scene, so I'm told; I wasn't there to defend myself, unfortunately. Why he should jump to the conclusion that *I* had put it there, goodness only knows.

The Quartermaster refuses to have it in his store, and the boiler-house seems to be locked every time I try it, so I have ordered two men to push the infernal thing under one of the huts and cover it with cinders. There seems to be no other way out. Of course I intend this to be only a temporary measure.

FRIDAY, 28 MARCH 1941

The question of the disposal of the rubber tubing is settled. Apparently the cookhouse fatigue men use it to wash down the cookhouse floor and so on, and it ought never to have been moved. No one told me this at the time, of course, or I might have been spared a great deal of worry and bother. So it is now back where it started, as I found out quite by accident this morning. I tripped over it, as a matter of fact, on my way back after inspecting the cookhouse.

Another note from Rawlinson by the afternoon

post to say that Poole's trousers caught fire during the first period after 'break' yesterday. I must write for details, as I believe there is more in this than meets the eye. Poole was never quite enough of a disciplinarian, to my mind.

15 JULY 1941

A tallish sergeant came into the office this morning while I was reading a Command Order about hair-slides (A.T.S.) and said he was Scringe.

I did not follow what he meant. 'How do you mean?' I asked. 'Are you unwell?'

He said he was Sergeant Scringe.

'Do you mean your name is Scringe?' I asked him, raising my eyebrows. It seemed to me a most extraordinary thing, though I remember a boy called Hasty, now I come to think of it, in the Upper Fourth and rather good at Greek. Not that this chap looked as if he would be much use at Greek, I must say – or Latin either for that matter. Still, there it is.

'Yes, sir, Sergeant Scringe,' he said. 'Scringe is my name and I'm a sergeant, sir – by rank of course.'

'Well, what else would you be a sergeant by?' I said – 'Royal proclamation? Or what?' I had an idea the fellow meant to be insolent, and I immediately asked him for his number and pretended to write it down in Command Orders, not having any other paper handy. I make a point of asking N.C.O.s for their numbers if they show any tendency to be truculent. It brings it home to them, I think.

Collingridge used to do the same thing at Burgrove (which still stands in its own grounds in spite of the bombs, as Gilbert said in his last letter. He always had a clever way of putting things, though the Head told me once – however, I detest gossip, and after all it's what a man *is* rather than what he *has* been that counts. Though both are important, of course.). I don't mean Collingridge used to ask the boys for their numbers, because naturally they hadn't any, except on their lockers in the boot-room and so on; it was a help with the washing and mending, Matron said. He used to ask them their ages instead: '*How* old are you, Fearnly? Ten? Dear me, I should have thought eight was nearer the mark.' He always said it worked very well, but I don't know. Boys are curious creatures.

I tried it myself once or twice, but not very successfully. Mason said, I remember, that in another eight years he would be twice as old as his father was fifty years ago, and naturally I couldn't make any comment in case it might appear to be a reflection on Mr Mason in some way. The *first* Mr Mason that would be, of course, not that the second Mr Mason's name would be Mason at all, now I come to think of it. Every master has his own way of dealing with boys, I suppose. Mine, I like to think, is to lead rather than drive.

I was thinking rather nostalgically of the old

days and the smell of the hymn-books in chapel and mark-reading and so on and so forth, when the phone rang and a voice said, 'You're through.'

'Through where?' I asked.

'Hold on a moment,' the operator said. 'I'm just getting them for you.'

'Getting *who*?' I said. 'I haven't asked for anybody.'

Then a man's voice said, 'You're very faint. Can you hear me?' and somebody else asked me whether I was long distance. Of course I couldn't say without knowing where they were speaking from, and I was pointing this out when the telephone made a loud jarring noise and drowned me.

'Wentworth here,' I said.

'Hullo!' said the man's voice.

'Hullo!' I said, 'Wentworth here.'

'Hullo!' said the man.

'Hul*lo*!' I said. 'Wentworth speaking.'

'Hullo! Hullo!' said the man.

'This is Crowsfoot double-two-owe-nine-ah,' I said carefully.

'Speak up Crowsfoot,' said the operator, 'they're calling you.'

I was on the verge of losing patience when the phone on the Adjutant's desk began to ring, so I shouted, 'Hold on a moment,' and hurried across. It is always the way when the Adjutant goes out.

'Hullo!' I said, snatching up the receiver.

'Wentworth here,' said a voice.

I could hardly believe my ears.

'Hullo!' I said, 'Hullo! Hul-LO! Who is it? What is going on here?'

'Hullo !' said the man.

'Look here,' I said. 'Were you speaking to me on the other phone just now?'

'The *other* phone? What do you mean?' he said.

'I'm speaking on two phones,' I explained.

'No need to do that,' he said. 'There's a mouthpiece and receiver all in one piece on these new models. You're only giving yourself unnecessary trouble.'

'Oh, go and boil yourself!' I cried, tired of all this tomfoolery. Then I slammed the receiver down and went back to my own desk.

The telephone there was still crackling.

'Wentworth here,' I said wearily.

'Can you take a call from Bicester, sir?' asked the operator.

'I can take a call from Honolulu if there isn't a raving lunatic on the other end,' I said bitterly. However, it turned out to be the C.O. and I apologized at once, in case he had misunderstood what I had said to the operator.

'What's that, Wentworth?' he said.

'I said I was sorry I said I could take a call from Honolulu if there wasn't a raving lunatic on the other end, sir,' I said.

'What the devil d'you mean, Wentworth?' he said.

I saw I had made a mistake in bringing the wretched business up at all. But there was nothing for it but to go on with it, now it had started. 'I was speaking on two phones, sir,' I explained, 'and I couldn't make head or tail of either of them. There seemed to be a complete fool on the line – '

'There often is,' said the C.O.

'So, naturally, when the operator asked me if I could take a call from Bicester I said – jokingly, sir – that I could take one from Honolulu, provided – '

'Well, don't say it again,' said the C.O., who seemed to be in one of his testy moods. 'Send a car for me at 16.30.'

As usual in this office there was no pencil or paper for me to take the message down, and I was obliged to strike a match and make a note on the blotting-paper with the burnt end. I must remember to speak to my clerk about this absurd shortage of pencils. There is no excuse for it whatever as far as I can see. We were never short of pencils at Burgrove.

As a matter of fact as soon as I had finished my note I caught sight of a pencil under the filing-cabinet, of all places, and had to go down on my hands and knees to fish it out. Imagine my annoyance when I got to my feet to see a tallish sergeant watching me from the opposite side of the desk.

'Well?' I said, flushing. 'What do *you* want?'

He said he was Scringe.

I simply couldn't follow what the fellow meant.

22 JULY 1941

Today started badly. The C.O. complained about the jam at breakfast again, and said the toast was burnt. I do my best but really I cannot be expected to make marmalade out of thin air. Nor do I see what the fact that they have kidneys twice a week at the R.A.S.C. Mess has to do with it. They must be lucky, I suppose. As I said, there is a war on and we must just do the best we can. The Colonel became so unpleasant that I decided to change the subject and began to talk to Roberts, our Adjutant here, about Part II Orders, which I am very anxious to get clear in my head.

'By the way, Roberts,' said the Colonel suddenly, 'Major Bolt was talking to me yesterday about a Sergeant he's got down there – String, Singe – some name like that. Know anything about him?'

'Never heard of him, sir.'

'Scringe,' I said. 'Sergeant Scringe, sir. He came to see me the other day.'

'When was this, Wentworth?'

'The day you were out – you were over at Bicester, I think, sir.'

'The day the car I ordered failed to turn up, you mean, eh?' said the Colonel grimly.

'My pencil had rolled under the filing-cabinet, sir,' I explained, 'and unfortunately the note I made was not very legible, with the result that instead of 16.30 hours – '

'I know, I know,' said the Colonel in his short-
tempered way. 'You had been reading a book about
Waterloo so you sent the car to Wellington at 18.15.
Never mind that now. What did this fellow Scringe
want?'

'He didn't say, sir.'

'Well, did you ask him?'

The fact is I was very busy at the time Sergeant
Scringe came in. I was speaking on two telephones,
which distracted my attention, and what is more I
didn't care very much for the man's manner. With
a little encouragement I believe he would have
become insolent. So I sent him away with a flea in
his ear.

The C.O. is a fine type of soldier. I would follow
him anywhere, though as a matter of fact he prefers
to be on his own when he is inspecting and so on.
But if he has a fault it is a lack of patience with
people who have had less experience of army life
and ways than he has. After all, if he were to join
the staff at Burgrove, I dare say he would find
himself a bit out of his depth for a term or two and
glad enough to take an occasional tip from an old-
stager like myself. The boot would be on the other
leg there, I fancy. I shall never forget Collingridge's
first term, when he walked across the piece of lawn
in front of the Headmaster's study. Of course
nobody had told him, so he was not really to blame
in any way. I only mean that that is the sort of thing

that can easily happen to anyone in those particular circumstances. It isn't quite the same thing as my forgetting to ask Sergeant Scringe what he wanted, but the analogy is close enough to show what I mean.

The C.O. and Roberts were still talking about this wretched Sergeant when I left them and went across to the office. But I soon forgot him in the normal routine of the day.

French was the first to ring up.

'Look here,' he said, 'about this A/16 of yours.'

'Yes,' I said. 'Which A/16 is that?'

(An A/16 is a thing we attach or 'subjoin', as we say, to a letter, so that the other man can tear it off and send it back to show he has had the letter it was subjoined to. If he doesn't send it, then of course we know he hasn't had it and can send him another, or have a Court of Inquiry, as the case may be.)

'Dated the fifth,' French said.

'Yes, yes. But what was it attached to?'

'It wasn't attached to anything.'

'Well, subjoined then.'

'It wasn't subjoined either. It was all by itself.'

I saw at once that there had been some mistake. Naturally one doesn't send an A/16 entirely on its own, because even if it were returned it would not prove that anything had arrived – except the A/16, of course, and even that would have come back.

'Well,' I began, 'it's a most extraordinary thing' – and then I had an idea. 'You're not talking about a *message* with a *reference number* A/16 by any chance, are you, French?' I asked.

He said he was, and that of course explained the whole thing. We might have wasted the entire morning if I hadn't happened to hit on the only possible explanation. After that it was all more or less plain sailing. French complained that our A/16 dated the fifth cancelled our A/9 dated the third and that this in turn had cancelled our A/178 dated the twenty-fifth. He said he wouldn't have minded that, only our A/178 was in fact a cancellation of our letter number four-three oblique one-three-seven oblique A of 12th May, and he wanted to know where he stood.

'It's all perfectly simple, French,' I said. 'This four-three oblique letter was cancelled on the twenty-fifth, then it was uncancelled, and now the uncancelling has been cancelled so that the letter itself is cancelled again. Is that all right?'

'But then,' he said, 'that means there's nothing left.'

'No,' I said. 'The episode is finished.'

'You mean you don't want any nominations for the West Indies after all?'

'No,' I said. 'No, I don't think so. No. Had you got somebody you wanted to nominate?'

'No,' he said. 'Only I don't see what happens to your four-three oblique two-four-nine oblique A dated 8th June in that case.'

'Does it matter?' I asked.

123

He said no, he supposed it didn't, and after a word or two about things in general he rang off. French is a good officer, but he tends to fuss rather a lot about non-essentials. After all, if a thing is cancelled it is cancelled and that is all there is to be said about it. Poor old Poole took to reading through his old mark-lists in his last term or two, which I always thought rather an unhealthy sign. It's the same sort of thing in a way.

All the same, it's as well to be certain, so I rang for my clerk and told him to hunt up a letter we had written about vacancies for suitable N.C.O.s in the West Indies.

'It's in the Equipment File,' he said. 'Four-three oblique – '

'In the Equipment File!' I cried. 'What in the name of goodness is it doing in the Equipment File?'

'It's Captain Stevens' system, sir.'

Captain Stevens was Adjutant here before Captain Trevelyan, who was succeeded by the present man, Roberts.

'But Captain Trevelyan abolished all that and started a system of his own,' I objected.

'Yes, sir, but when Captain Roberts came he said that of the two he preferred Captain Stevens' system. He said it only meant looking through fifty-six files instead of a hundred-and-ninety.'

Of course I couldn't permit a lance-bombardier to say anything that appeared to criticize something an officer had done, so I sent Hotfoot (another curious name) about his business and settled down to the work of entering up the secret mail.

A Colonel Ferris came to lunch. He is something to do with National Economy, though I must say he ate a good deal. Still, he wears his trousers very short, which sets a good example, I suppose.

He asked me what we did with our old pen-nibs, and I said we wrote letters with them. It seemed to satisfy him.

12 AUGUST 1942

I am to go to a new regiment tomorrow – the 600th. I should call it 'X' or 'B' Regiment normally, for security reasons, but this unit happens to be known simply as 'X' Regiment (another letter, really, of course, but the meaning is clear, I hope), so I thought it safer to reverse the procedure and call it a number. One has to be particularly careful what one says when moving.

It is unsettling somehow to make a change after all this time, but I suppose a soldier must be prepared to up sticks and be off to the end of the world if need be. It is not that I mind, only one gets used to having the hole in the carpet on the right-hand side of the fire-place in the mess and it is disconcerting for the first day or two in the new mess to find it on the left. I have got used to the filing system here, too, in a way, and there is the barber in Leopold Street – quite exceptionally good and very moderate. Goodness knows what the local man at Salisbury will be like.

The C.O. has been most kind. I am not actually appointed Adjutant of the new unit, he says, but it will be only a matter of days, he thinks.

13 AUGUST 1942

Well, here I am, with very mixed feelings I must say, particularly as I am not where I expected to be, but somewhere quite different. At least I don't think I am expected to be here, unless I made a foolish mistake in the first place, which does not seem very likely.

The trouble began at the booking-office, where I put down my railway warrant saying 'Crowsfoot' to the clerk – forgetting for the moment that it was Crowsfoot *from* which I was going, not *to* which. The clerk, with a rather impudent grin, said, 'Return?' and somebody in the queue asked me if my journey was really necessary. I made no reply, but merely stood quietly waiting for my ticket to be made out. It was all the more annoying to find that the ticket, when at last I got it, was made out to the wrong destination.

'Look here,' I said. 'I want to go to Salisbury. You've given me a ticket to Bury St Edmunds.'

'It says Bury St Edmunds here,' he said, showing me the warrant, and to my amazement I found that it did.

'There has been some mistake,' I began.

'Your parents', not mine,' said the clerk – a remark of which I could make neither head nor tail. Surely he did not suppose that my warrant had been made out by my father, even had he been still alive, which, as a matter of fact, he is not? Of course the clerk could not know that, but still! One does not have warrants made out by one's parents, dead *or* alive.

Unfortunately the train came in while I was wondering what to do, leaving me no time to ring up my old headquarters and make certain where I was supposed to go. I still think the C.O. said Salisbury, but on the other hand there it was in black and white on the warrant, 'Bury St Edmunds', so rather than risk turning up late at my new unit, which creates a bad impression, I decided to jump in.

I suppose the difficulty over my ticket had muddled me, for it was not until the train had pulled out that I remembered I had forgotten to make arrangements about my luggage. I suppose it will go to Salisbury as it was labelled there, unless it stays at Crowsfoot. In any case it is extremely awkward to be in this place in borrowed pyjamas, quite apart from shaving and so on. One feels such a fool.

There were two young subalterns in my carriage who were most helpful after I had explained my troubles to them. I was doubtful at first of the wisdom of telling them where I was going until one of them said he was a spy and the other offered to take off his vest and show me the marks of the parachute harness on his back, at which we all laughed.

'What would that prove?' I asked. 'Germans use parachutes as well, you know.'

'But haven't you seen the film?' said one of them, staring.

'What film?' I asked.

'*Next of Kin*.'

'No,' I said. 'But I've heard of it, of course.'

'Good for you. Only I thought you must have seen it when you laughed.'

'Seen it when I laughed?' I said. 'Oh, I see. You mean you thought I must have laughed when I saw it. But then I haven't seen it, as I told you.'

'No, no. What I mean is I thought you wouldn't have laughed if you hadn't seen it – '

'Naturally not,' I said. 'One doesn't laugh at what one doesn't see, does one?' He seemed a particularly incoherent young man, even as young men go today, and I turned to the other officer and asked him if he could tell me whether the 600th were at Bury St Edmunds.

He said he thought not, but believed the 500th were at a place called Parkinghurst or used to be, if that was any help. In any case, he said, the train didn't go to Bury St Edmunds or anywhere near it. This final blow quite disheartened me and in the end I decided to make the best of a bad business and get out at Parkinghurst. Rather a dull sergeant at the drill hall seemed to think I had come to pay the men, but in the end I made myself understood and he agreed to take me to see the Major.

To my amazement and, I am bound to say, distress, I found myself face to face with a man who was once, for a short time, a colleague of mine at Burgrove. In the ordinary way, naturally, I am delighted to meet old members of the staff, but Major Faggott – well really, sometimes I pretty nearly lost patience with his *laissez faire* attitude and his almost *roistering* way of going on. Not a good scholar either. However, there it was.

'Well, well, well,' he said. 'Ruffle my periwig if it isn't old Wentworth, the doyen of Burgrove. Have a whisky and tell me what brings you here. I suppose you still drink as heavily as ever?'

'I am on my way to join the 600th,' I replied, ignoring his last remark, 'and I thought I would report here –'

'This is the 500th,' he said.

'I know,' I said, 'but unfortunately I got into the wrong train for Bury St Edmunds –'

'Bury St Edmunds!' said Major Faggott (he never scrupled to interrupt in the old days, I remember). 'But the 600th aren't at Bury St Edmunds. All this is very peculiar, Wentworth. I am inclined to think you are a deserter.'

The fool then warned me that anything I said

would be taken down in triplicate and used in evidence against me, and asked me what I had done with my luggage.

'I have sent it to Salisbury,' I said shortly.

'An excellent plan. Then when you get posted to a unit in Newcastle and take the wrong train for Haverfordwest you'll find your luggage waiting for you. The only thing is, what are you going to do in the meantime?'

'If you will direct me to a hotel,' I began, rather stiffly – but Major Faggott would not hear of it, and very generously offered me a bed and the loan of a pair of pyjamas. They are rather more gaudy than my usual choice, as one would expect, but it would have been churlish to refuse. I am sure he means well, but, well, I suppose we have rather different ideas of what is and what is *not* done.

14 AUGUST 1942

We must wait and see what the morrow will bring forth. Major Faggott says I am to regard myself as attached here pending posting. 'We can always do with another officer,' he said at breakfast; 'it makes the messing easier.'

'But look here, sir,' I expostulated. 'I've been posted to the 600th. I really think I ought to be getting along.'

'I'll fix that,' he said. 'I'll speak to Charlie about you,' and explained in answer to my inquiry that Charlie was A.G.6. I did not quite like to say that I was unaware who or what A.G.6 might be, and was therefore obliged to let the matter drop. I suppose it is all right, but really it all seems a little irregular.

'What are we going to do with him?' asked the Major suddenly. 'We can't very well make him O.C. Transport, because there isn't any. At least, we could, of course, in case some comes along.'

'Gas Officer,' said a tall thin man who had just come in. 'Where's the *Mirror*?'

'By the way, this is Hobson — Wentworth. Hobson is my gunnery expert. You wouldn't think he had a glass eye, would you?'

'How do you do?' I said. 'I certainly shouldn't. In fact I can hardly tell the difference even now.'

'Very tactful,' said Faggott, slapping his leg and laughing like a madman. 'You've made a friend for life there, Wentworth. He says he can hardly tell the difference, Hobson, old boy. The same glassy look in each of them, eh? What?'

'I'm afraid I fail to see the joke, sir,' I said coldly. The fact is, the Major's laughter seemed to me to be in the worst possible taste. After all, one doesn't laugh at another man's infirmities.

'The joke is he hasn't got a glass eye,' said Faggott, rolling about in his chair in the most unseemly way. 'Which did you think it was? The dull-green one, or the one with all those red streaks in it? Oh, dear, oh, dear, Wentworth, you'll be the death of me yet. "Hardly tell the difference", wasn't it? I must make a note of that.'

'I'm afraid I know very little about gas, Hobson,' I said, to change the conversation. 'I mean, I should have to have a course of instruction before I could conscientiously take on the appointment.'

However, Hobson assured me that that wouldn't be necessary. 'This is a new unit, you see,' he explained. 'Just forming. So nobody knows anything about anything. You'll just have to pick it up as you go along.'

'Like a crossing-sweeper,' added Major Faggott, with his usual lack of taste.

Apparently my first duty as Gas Officer is to go up in an aeroplane. I was rather surprised at this, naturally, for I failed to see the connexion, but Major Faggott explained that we had been ordered to send an observer on an air co-operation exercise and I was the obvious person to go. He said he believed, as a matter of fact, that the message was intended for another unit, but it had come to us so we must just carry out instructions.

'But I have never flown,' I objected.

'It's quite easy,' said Hobson. 'You just get in and sit still and then you get out again when you get back to the ground – '

'Or sooner, as the case may be,' said Faggott.

'You won't be expected to take the controls,' added Hobson. 'The R.A.F. have undertaken to provide a qualified driver.'

'Pilot,' I corrected, *sotto voce*.

15 August 1942

It has been a most interesting experience. The exercise was at night, which I hadn't expected, so that one was unable to see the ground; but, of course, it was the same for the pilot and the rest of the crew, so I must not grumble.

The R.A.F. were most kind. They gave me a parachute before we started and explained how I was to use it. 'You probably won't have to,' my pilot told me, 'unless there are hostiles about and we get pranged.'

'Pranged?' I said.

'Yes.'

'I see,' I said, though I confess I did not quite follow what he meant.

'In that case, just nip out, count three slowly and pull this thing.'

'Right,' I said briskly. 'Does one come down with much of a bump?'

'Oh, no,' he said. 'Unless the parachute fails to open.'

'I see,' I said.

It is not very easy to get into a bomber at night, and unfortunately, when I had got in, there was no seat for me and I had to squat on my parachute.

'By the way,' said the pilot, when we were all inside, 'you've come as an observer, haven't you?'

'Yes,' I said. 'Yes, yes.'

'What are you going to observe, particularly?'

'Well,' I said, 'nothing particularly. Just general

observation.' The fact is nobody had remembered to tell me what I was supposed to be doing.

'Afraid you won't see much tonight,' he said. 'Except the stars.'

'It doesn't matter, thanks,' I said. 'I'm a Gas Officer, really. At least, I hope to be when I have had a little more experience.'

'I see,' said the pilot.

Soon after that he started up the engines and conversation ceased. It is rather noisy in a bomber when the engines are going – 'revving', as they say – and one has to shout to make oneself heard.

'How high are we now?' I shouted, when we had been roaring along for about five minutes. It is quite impossible to get any idea of height when you are flying in the dark.

'We haven't started yet,' shouted the pilot. 'I'm just warming her up.'

'Oh,' I said, feeling rather a fool. I suppose in the noise and darkness I had got rather confused.

However, it was much the same when we did start, except that one had to shout rather louder. The machine was very steady, and after a time I became more used to the noise and began to get ready to observe. Then, without any warning, there was a sudden bump and the aeroplane dropped like a lift.

I kept my head, and turned inquiringly to the pilot.

'Pranged?' I shouted. But he shook his head and said, 'Cloud.'

'I see,' I cried, but I don't think he heard me.

Nothing happened for another ten minutes and I began to grow aware that my seat was far from comfortable. By pure ill-chance, in endeavouring to adjust the parachute on which I was sitting, I caught hold of the wrong handle and something came right away in my hand. I rose to a crouching position and, turning round to see what was amiss, was horrified to see a volume of white material, like dough, pouring out of the wrapping. I did not know what to do and the pilot, not realizing my predicament, added to my difficulties by turning the machine abruptly on its side so that I was thrown off my balance and forced to put out a hand to save myself. Instantly there was a sharp report and some kind of flare or firework was projected from the underside of the aeroplane.

The pilot said something which I did not catch, for I had my hands too full at the moment to attend to him. It is a skilled task, I am informed, to repack a parachute in the most favourable conditions, and I do not believe it can be done in a crouching position in an aeroplane in the dark. There is a great deal of material to cope with, for one thing.

My great fear was that the thing would master me and spread all over the aircraft so that we should all be choked or, if not that, that the pilot would no longer be able to see the controls. It seemed to spring up after me the moment I rose from a sitting position, and do what I would, folds and loops of the stuff kept oozing out from under me at the sides and back.

'Sit tight,' I said to myself, 'and keep your nerve', and I remember thinking what a story this would make to tell to the boys, if ever I should get back to the old life at Burgrove. I think this helped to steady me.

Suddenly I felt a tap on my shoulder and carefully turning about I found that the navigator was trying to communicate with me.

'What do you say?' I cried. 'I can't hear you.'

'Your shirt's hanging out at the back,' he roared.

I realized then that the parachute had got hitched to my Sam Browne, which I had put on for the flight, and it was this, of course, that had given it a tendency to rise up in the air when I moved. I unhitched it and had practically no further trouble, I am thankful to say.

'I am afraid you were too busy to observe much,' said the pilot when we landed.

'Not at all,' I said. 'It has been a most interesting experience for me.'

'It has for all of us,' he said, which I thought very nice of him. After all, one flight more or less in a bomber, even at night, is all in the day's work for its gallant crew.

[There is, of course, a vast mass of material in the war-time diaries from which I might quote. But this is perhaps enough to show that my friend Wentworth

carried with him into the army those same qualities of solid worth and sound logical common sense that served him so well in his peacetime profession. Mr Wentworth returned to Burgrove after his demobilization in January 1946, and the Memorandum with which this book ends shows that he has lost little or nothing of his old flair for the big occasion.]

Memorandum from
A.J. Wentworth, BA

Sir – It is with considerable regret that I inform you that things cannot go on as they are at present unless some change is made. Had it been some small matter such as the school radiators, which have been stone cold for the last three days, I should have come to see you in the ordinary way, or the shortage of nibs and blotting-paper about which I have spoken fifty times to Rawlinson already, but it is *not*. A schoolmaster has plenty to do without that sort of thing in any case. But either there is discipline in a school or there is not. That is my point. And if there is no discipline I for one will have no part in it. I have not given up what might have been the best years of my life to Burgrove, in order to have my boot-laces tied to the legs of my desk at the end of it and so be prevented from rising to my feet when parents are shown into my classroom, as I always do. This is not the first time an attempt has been made to make me look ridiculous in front of other people, nor is it the last,

139

as I am well aware, after seeing Matron sneaking into your study this very afternoon with some garbled version no doubt of an incident outside the School Museum which could never have happened if people would stop misrepresenting my slightest action and making mare's nests at my expense out of nothing at all.

I have always done my best and put the interests of the school first, but if it is to be put about that I made an unprovoked attack with a cutlass on a boy of eleven years during the after-lunch rest-period, I can only say that the sooner I tender my resignation the better for all concerned. That the boy, Malcolm, was not even a member of my Mathematical Set would have been enough, one might have supposed, to scotch such a ridiculous story at the outset. But apparently it is not. The sword was not, as it happens, a cutlass, but a scimitar. There is no cutlass in the School Museum. But those who are responsible for spreading unfounded gossip of this kind about me are not likely to allow a trifle of that nature to stand in their way. I should be thankful, perhaps, that I am not accused of throwing assegais, of which a large number were presented to the school last term by Mr Tallboys and hang on the west wall at present, pending some other arrangement. He has also promised an elk's head and some West African wood-carvings.

I am determined to put a stop to this kind of

thing. I have as much right to handle the weapons in the Museum as anyone. More. The Museum is in my charge, as was settled at the Masters' Meeting in January, and Malcolm had no business to be there in the rest-period. Does Matron deny my right to take down the scimitar and dust it? If so, let her deny it to my face and I will very soon make clear to her where her jurisdiction ends and mine begins. She would be better employed in seeing that the boys are resting on their beds after lunch than in trying to interfere with the way I run the Museum.

I have little more to say. I consider that Malcolm's behaviour in dashing out of the Museum crying, 'Spare me! Spare me!' the moment he caught sight of me with the sword in my hand was little short of downright impertinence. The boy should be thrashed. That I should run after him to tell him to be quiet was not only a perfectly natural thing to do, it was my duty. And I shall continue to do my duty, with or without Matron's permission, for so long as I remain on the Staff here at Burgrove.

That that time is likely to be short we are both well aware. My resignation is in your hands. Should you wish to accept it, there is no more to be said, except to thank you for many happy years and much kindness and to ask you as a special favour that some arrangement be made to expedite the return of my laundry before I depart. I should of course in the ordinary way approach Matron on this matter, but you will understand, in the circumstances, that that is quite impossible. I have a few books which may be of use to the boys' library.

Should you desire me to withdraw my resignation I will do so, provided:

That a full apology is made by Matron in the presence of the whole Staff.

That Malcolm is thrashed, or otherwise punished at your discretion.

That other arrangements are made for the management of the School Museum, which it is now painful for me to enter.

I will take steps to deal with the comparatively trivial matter of the boot-laces myself.

(*Signed*) Arthur J. Wentworth

[*A copy of the note sent by the Headmaster to Wentworth, in answer to the foregoing Memorandum has come into my hands. It seems to clear the matter up.*]

FROM THE HEADMASTER

Dear A.J. – I don't know what all the fuss is about. Matron came to see me this afternoon about gym-shoes, not cutlasses.

I have seen Malcolm and told him not to be a silly little fool.

The man I had with me when I entered your classroom this morning was not a parent, or not, at any rate, in the sense in which we use the term; he had come to see about the breakdown in the central heating system. I cannot allow you to resign on the grounds that you were unable to stand up when a plumber came into your room.

So please put your personal feelings on one side – and remember, Wentworth, that the School must come first.

(*Signed*) G.S.

P.S. I have just completed arrangements for an old friend of yours, Major Faggott, to join us next term in Rawlinson's place. He will probably be willing to take over the Museum, if you really wish to give it up.

By all means use your own initiative about the boot-laces.